A Crew of One

Jeremy P. Tarcher / Putnam
a member of
Penguin Putnam Inc.
New York

A Crew of One

THE ODYSSEY OF A
SOLO MARLIN FISHERMAN

Carlos Bentos

Most Tarcher/Putnam books are available at special quantity
discounts for bulk purchases for sales promotions, premiums,
fund-raising, and educational needs. Special books or book
excerpts also can be created to fit specific needs. For details,
write Putnam Special Markets, 375 Hudson Street,
New York, NY 10014.

JEREMY P. TARCHER/PUTNAM
a member of
Penguin Putnam Inc.
375 Hudson Street
New York, NY 10014
www.penguinputnam.com

Library of Congress Cataloging-in-Publication Data

Bentos, Carlos.
    A crew of one : the odyssey of a solo marlin fisherman /
Carlos Bentos.
        p.   cm.
    ISBN 1-58542-154-5
    1. Marlin fishing—Anecdotes. 2. Bentos, Carlos.   I. Title.
SH691.M35 B46 2002   2001057361
799.1'778—dc21

Printed in the United States of America
10 9 8 7 6 5 4 3 2 1

This book is printed on acid-free paper. ∞

Book design by Deborah Kerner
"Marlin" illustration by Richard Waxberg

To my mother,
Margarita Yolanda

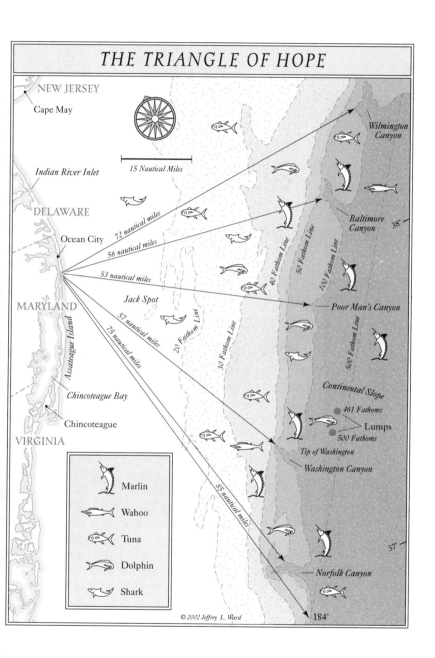

THE TRIANGLE OF HOPE

NEW JERSEY

Cape May

15 Nautical Miles

Indian River Inlet

DELAWARE

Ocean City

72 nautical miles

56 nautical miles

53 nautical miles

Jack Spot

MARYLAND

57 nautical miles

75 nautical miles

20 Fathom Line

30 Fathom Line

40 Fathom Line

50 Fathom Line

100 Fathom Line

500 Fathom Line

Assateague Island

Chincoteague Bay

Chincoteague

VIRGINIA

85 nautical miles

Wilmington Canyon

Baltimore Canyon

38°

Poor Man's Canyon

Continental Slope

461 Fathoms

500 Fathoms

Lumps

Tip of Washington

Washington Canyon

37°

Norfolk Canyon

184°

Marlin

Wahoo

Tuna

Dolphin

Shark

© 2002 Jeffrey L. Ward

Caribeña

CONTENTS

•

•

Carlos Bentos and Caribeña
COPYRIGHT © DALE TIMMONS, COASTAL FISHERMAN

We are all apprentices

in a craft where

no one ever becomes a master.

ERNEST HEMINGWAY

A Crew of One

.

.

LONG CASTS
FROM THE PAST

A fisherman and a light tackle angler, that is what I am. And a boatman, that is what I have become.

My life's journey—over a wandering course—spans almost sixty years of fishing, twenty-five of them in my native Uruguay. As a child, I was enthralled by the magic of fishing, drawn as if by romance. Side by side with my mother, my teacher, I caught my first fish at the age of three. But it wasn't until decades later, after I had exiled myself to a distant, different land, that I happened upon deep-sea fishing and the thrill of chasing and catching the elusive billfish. Seduced by the mystique of the great blue offshore world, I drifted away from the bucolic sandy beaches and the grassy banks of inland creeks. The deep, deep canyons sixty, eighty, one hundred miles from the Maryland coast of the Eastern United States became my new playing field.

Though all kinds of fishing are good and potentially rewarding, to me, nothing compares with the ultimate adventure of deep-sea trolling for billfish. Saltwater deep-sea fishing *is* the big time, the Major Leagues. Marlin are the apex of game fish. Catching one is like hitting a home run. They are hard to find and harder to hook. They combine the speed of the wahoo, the strength of the tuna, and the beauty of the mahimahi, but it's their mighty sword that makes them legendary and unique. The big blues can take half a day, or more, to subdue and bring to the boat. And they have an ineffable nobility that many of us who come in contact with them feel.

The marlin has come to be the essence and emblem of the world I love, that world far from land, where I have developed a profound respect for the power of the sea and the creatures in it. For almost twenty-five years now, I have been at the helm of my boat—most of the time alone, most of the time far offshore—searching for the elusive marlin, the target of choice in the sights of my fishing rod. In the highly competitive, close-knit world of marlin fishermen, I am an anomaly, a different guy: I speak English with a foreign accent—and constantly fish alone. Other marlin fishermen go out with larger, faster, better-equipped boats, manned by captains and mates, with four to six anglers on board (sometimes more!), all performing essential, specific tasks in order to make the boat go, hook fish, wire, perhaps tag, and gaff or release their prey. I, on the other hand, run my boat, plot the course, keep watch, and rig baits and fish all by myself. Far from land, there's no room for mistakes. Sloppiness or lack of attention can lead quickly to disaster. Perhaps it is this sense of complete engagement and immersion in the activity of fishing alone that I find so deeply satisfying.

The combination of my accent, my aloneness, my relative success in catching fish, and, lately, my age, must be what prompts my friends, acquaintances, and even strangers to compare me to Santiago—Hemingway's hero in *The Old Man and the Sea*. Flattering nonsense, of course, but I have to admit to a superficial similitude between me and, both the revered writer and the legendary Old Man. Like Hemingway's, my beard of thirty years is getting gray, and, like the Old Man, who fished alone forty-four days before his last epic battle, I battle the great fish by myself. As far as I know, no one has consistently fished alone far offshore, and certainly no one has been as lucky as the man from Uruguay.

I have been fortunate in raising my share of billfish, and lucky hooking up an unusually high percentage of them. At first, back in the late 1970s and early 1980s, most other marlin fishermen thought I was crazy. And I understood. "Saltwater offshore angling is a team sport..." wrote the authoritative Peter Goadby in his old book *Big Fish and Blue Water*. But one day, just answering the call of the sea, I decided to try it alone. Twenty-some years ago, I set out into the vast Atlantic and caught a marlin. That very first day, I proved it could be done! After having that big ocean all to myself, I knew I would never enjoy the "traditional" method of fishing big game with a team as much as fishing alone.

"But aren't there risks involved?" some ask. It's true, when I am fishing alone, I am, perhaps, too far from shore with no help in sight, during storms, when I'm handling my boat alone in big seas ... when I'm hauling in a marlin that is perfectly capable of stabbing me with his sword or pulling me overboard. How can I write this without thinking of Chris Bowie being fatally pulled over the gunwales of the old *Trophy Box* by a marlin of less than 200 pounds? What I answer when others ask, "Aren't you afraid ... what if something goes wrong?" is, no, I am not afraid, and not because I am that valiant, but because I believe in fate.

For centuries, countless boats and lives have been lost at sea—many the red-eyed lover weeping on shore. But, so far, I have been spared that flick of *mala suerte,* bad luck that has randomly doomed so many who venture to sea. Make no mistake: fishing offshore for big fish is a dangerous game even with an experienced crew, and, yet, in spite of the perils, I know of no greater challenge and pleasure.

Every time Santiago left the Havana harbor in his crude skiff to fish the Gulf Stream off the Cuban coast, he did so compelled by the urgency of the most basic human needs: the need to work, the need to eat, the need to survive. Piloting my aging boat *Caribeña* off the Maryland coast, I never kill billfish, and rarely kill any other pelagic game. I release my fish alive back into the sea. I do not fish for a living: I live to fish. For me, this is what gives meaning to the sport. I believe the true satisfaction of fishing comes from feeling mentally and physically at one with the prey. It's not the having; it's the getting that counts.

Since I bought and equipped my own boats, first *Pica Olas*, an Egg Harbour 33′, and then the *Caribeña*, a Bertram 35′, I have escaped the glad-handing life, the public persona of a restaurant owner and a radio announcer and fled to the ocean, to retreat, eat frugally, be mute for hours, and occasionally talk to myself. In so doing, I have learned to be alone, and more than that—I have reaffirmed my appreciation, even my growing need, for solitude. Other than being a monk and retiring into a cave to meditate, nothing beats fishing alone far offshore for deep introspection, coming to know oneself, and feeling attuned to nature, the elements, our place in this universe.

I have known many forms of solitude: fishing and reading in my youth; the self-exile of living in a country not my own; the isolation of being surrounded by a strange language; and the soothing silence that comes from living alone. I find solitude both a comfort and a challenge. And nowhere is it as perfect as when I am out for a day of marlin fishing in *Caribeña*, or even better during an overnight trip, when all things are possible—including disaster—and both achieving victory and avoiding misadventure are solely in my hands.

Releasing almost all the fish I catch is not just compassion; it is also common sense. White marlin, blue marlin, and sailfish are not only under intense environmental pressure—

like pollution and global warming—but, even worse, they are the accidental by-catch in extensive and intensive commercial fishing operations that continually push the stocks to a dangerous low, so I don't want to add to the woes of these beautiful creatures and drive them closer to the endangered species list. I choose to fight them as fairly as I can on their own "turf" in a contest of equals. If and when I win the match, I release the fish to fight again another day.

As often as I can, I tag my fish and send my reports to the Southeast Fisheries Science Center for its Cooperative Game Fish Tagging Program, which is run under the auspices of NOAA (National Oceanic and Atmospheric Administration) and the U.S. Department of Commerce. I also tag marlin for the Billfish Foundation. Tagging enables scientists to track recaptured marlin and learn about their migratory patterns and life span. It's amazing how much we still don't know: marlin are essentially mysterious creatures, wilder than lions and tigers whose habits are well known. This is one of the fascinations of marlin fishing: while most wild animals have been largely relegated to game preserves, the marlin roams over vast distances, unconstrained, uncircumscribed, making its living precisely in the same way it has for several million years. It roams our last great wilderness, the blue offshore water, fathoms upon fathoms deep, a place owned by no nation, without boundaries or borders and no fixed habitation for man.

In falling under the spell of the marlin, I am not alone.

Catching this fish, the king of the ocean, is the dream of millions of fishermen in this country alone. What lures us to the sport is the twin thrill of the hunt itself and the surroundings in which it is carried out. The contest is creature to creature, and the creatures are well matched. In the case of a mountain trout, the angler confronts an instinctively wily creature adept at survival, a highly evolved escape artist operating in a relatively shallow world of hidden nooks and crannies. But in the case of deep-sea billfish, the angler confronts speed, power, the brute force of a torpedo-shaped animal whose ascendancy over other creatures of the deep awakes that primal urge to meet the beast. Man to beast, the competition can make for a battle of heroic proportions and high drama on the high seas.

I have sought out this place far from shore, the deep blue water where I feel myself most human, most alive, and particularly most aware of my physical vulnerability and my true fortitude. I have sought out the elemental struggle against nature, where we pit our wits, strength, and will against something larger and stronger than we are. This book is about the immense beauty I have found there, the perils, and the joy.

Let me welcome you aboard, invite you to thumb through my nautical yarns and test the strength of my lines and their knots. I will share with you what I know about the adventures of fishing for marlin in solitude.

Buen viaje. Enjoy the ride.

FISHING THE OCEANS
OF MY MIND

At five knots, it took me almost a whole day to arrive at the indigo current I had been hoping to find long before sunset. White-feathered breasts of gliding Cory's shearwaters and the flickering wings of small black petrels had first caught my eye; then ripples announced an impending change. A westerly eddy of the warm water of the Gulf Stream, flowing up from the south, had finally moved in to pierce the colder green water of the Labrador Current, sweeping down from the north. Nomadic waters collided in colorful silence, four or five hundred yards off *Caribeña*'s starboard bow. The sea surface temperature gradually increased from 76 to 77.5 degrees, tripping the alarm of my depth finder, a Raytheon V 8110.

Excited, I scaled the ladder connecting cockpit and flying bridge; fast feet alternating the seven narrow teak steps, sure hands sliding up the inclined aluminum rails. I silenced the temperature alarm and registered my location in case I wanted to return. According to my marine chart, I was close to the 500-fathom line off the Norfolk Canyon, eighty miles off the Virginia shore, trolling in 3,500 feet of water, the bottom of the ocean a full kilometer beneath *Caribeña*'s black hull.

I swung *Caribeña* around, and set her on automatic pilot at five knots, running parallel to a patchy line of sargasso weed, a free-floating yellow-brown plant that extends for miles along the many inner currents, forming the seams of the stream. Weed lines are the fertile "flat forests" of the ocean, rich with plankton, a magnet for small fish that in turn often attract large pelagics like marlin.

Back on deck, I checked to make sure that none of the four baits I was trolling had picked up any weed. It felt good to have found this site without the assistance of temperature charts prepared from satellite imaging. I sensed a good omen. Judging from the height of the sun, I guessed it was 4:00. I scanned the horizon with binoculars, picking out two orange buoys that marked a commercial long-liner's set. Each set is thirty to forty miles of 700-pound test line, armed with 4,000 hooks dangling from as many leaders, each carrying a Cyalume Lightstick that glows green or blue to attract fish. The long-liners were after swordfish and tuna, but each set is a death trap, killing scores of untargeted fish, mainly white and blue marlin in their by-catch. The long-liners would be back at night to haul in their bounty.

Earlier, I had heard on the VHF marine channels of my radio that several white marlin had been caught in a similar break, probably by Norfolk or Virginia Beach sportfishing boats, since I didn't recognize the voices of the captains or the names of their vessels. I listened in but didn't talk to them—never do. I like to keep a low profile unless I have something important to say about fishing or weather conditions that I judge they ought to know.

"I just let one go. I'm one for four," reported one captain.

"We raised three and missed them all."

"Marlin?"

"Yup. Three whites."

"Lose those rubber hooks!" said a third voice.

"How many you seen, Johnny?"

"Saw two. We're two for two," came fast the happy answer, and then with a disappointed tone: "but we missed a nice blue after that. I thought we had him good. . . ."

I could almost touch his disappointment, his sense of failure. The guy was in pain. The two whites caught couldn't make him forget the big blue he had lost, which could have been the only blue that had chased his bait in several years.

"That you, by the tanker?"

"Yes, sir. To its starboard side."

"Thought so. By the six-twenty line?"

"Yeah."

That was the key information I had been hoping to hear: the 620 line, which referred to the horizontal or "bottom" line of the Loran grid overlapped on the charts we use to locate any point in the ocean. I already knew that someone had hooked a white marlin at 500 fathoms, but I hadn't known how far south. The 620 line pinpointed the location where the fish were showing up. I entered this new destination in the Loran and kept *Caribeña*'s southerly course.

On the way, I switched my radio to the weather channel; a hurricane was beginning to creep up from the south. It was still some 800 hundred miles southeast off Hatteras, packing winds of more than 100 miles per hour, but fortunately moving at a very slow pace. For the next twenty-four hours, I was in no danger of being caught in angry seas, but the disturbance to the south could already be felt in the long swells, each three football fields in length and thirty feet high, over which *Caribeña* rode. Given the promise of white marlin lurking in the cobalt depths of the Gulf Stream, the relative calm of the seas, and the late afternoon hour, rather than returning to port I decided to stay overnight. The evening would be good for fishing, the night good for the soul.

White marlin are leery hunters and finicky eaters, so I put on fresh baits. Four ballyhoos, two pulled from the short rigger positions, and two from the long riggers' pins. As always, my daisy chain of five six-inch rubber squids performed its animated dance while being pulled from a rod-and-reel set in the rod holder on the transom's starboard side.

Within minutes of trolling the warm edge of the sargasso weed line, the starboard short rigger bait was slammed by a small mahimahi. It jumped, a twelve-pound fish with a big blunt head, its body tapering like an inverted arrowhead toward its tail, its back emerald green, its flanks an intense yellow with hundreds of blue and purple spots.

"Dinner for one!" I said to myself, as I reeled him in without touching or entangling any of the other three lines, keeping the boat under way at minimum speed, hoping the baits and the daisy chain would entice another bite. But no fish showed up, and in minutes I had the dolphin fish on board.

Having had the overnight trip in the back of my mind, I had come prepared: lemons to squeeze; tomatoes to dice; one medium red onion—half to be chopped and half to be sliced as garnishing rings; garlic—to be finely minced; the aromatic cilantro that I like so much—to be chopped *sans* the stems; and those two short, thick, dark-green jalapeño peppers on the galley's countertop. Just eyeing them had made me cringe. So I would use only one—without the seeds.

"Now let's fool the marlin," I said. I replaced the ballyhoo that the mahimahi had mauled. My baits swam well, and I altered course, pulling away from the weed line. I wanted marlin not dorado chasing my ballyhoos.

I filleted the dorado on top of the Igloo cooler. Long, short, and shallow cuts followed by swift, striping pulls from the top of each flank left the fish's skin in my hands. I sliced the fillets, cut them in pieces, and immersed them in lemon juice and the chopped melange I had prepared. I buried the bowl in ice. Fresh seviche, cold and *picante!* How to contain my sudden hunger until the fish was properly "cooked," in its marination, which would take a few hours? My empty stomach rumbled, but I momentarily fooled it with a few bites of Muenster cheese.

Santiago had dined on raw mahimahi to keep up his strength in the middle of his marathon battle with the giant marlin. Like the Old Man, I had caught a dolphin. But, unlike him, I wouldn't be eating mahimahi raw as he did in the grip of hunger during his overnight ordeal.

"What an excellent fish dolphin is to eat cooked," Santiago had said. "And what a miserable fish raw. I will never go in a boat again without salt or limes." The old Man was afraid that the raw dorado could be emetic and affect his strength. I learned my lesson from that page of his book: be prepared.

I managed to keep my paws off the seviche, munching instead on delicious cilantro leaves as my eyes played a sort of tic-tac-toe game with the skipping and swimming baits. I relaxed, leaning against the ladder, bare chested, the sun warming my skin, wondering, when, suddenly, it appeared— a white marlin's distinctive black dorsal fin, frenetic, determined, pursuing the erratic splash-shine-dive-swim-splash-shine again of my closest silvery ballyhoo, the hook-rigged, eight-inch-long bait barely ahead of the charging billfish.

"Here it is!" I said aloud, jumping toward the rod. The fish was a mere twenty feet from the transom of my trolling boat. As always, my heart pumped hard. I live for this moment—the marlin strike.

I plucked the rod from its holder, thumbed the line, and put the Shimano-20 reel in free spool. The marlin surged forward, bill out of the water, eyes zeroed in on the escaping ballyhoo. The imminence of the white's strike was well advertised by its surge and its amazing color change: the dull dark-brown colors of the marlin's slender body turned a copperish blue. Its dorsal and pectoral fins and bill all glowed with an electric blue, the marlin's trademark preceding the final assault. This majestic fish was "lit up," as we say, an explosion of colors reflecting its brutal excitement, blood lust, and raw hunger, the natural endowments of its predatory rank.

A powerful kick of its tail and the white's long pointed spear flipped sideways, bashing the bait. This is the normal approach billfish employ to stun their prey, which, after the blow, floats inert or sinks slowly. I instantly dropped back, letting the line flow free from the reel, allowing the "stunned" bait to float exactly where the blow had occurred. The fish grabbed the bait in its jaws, unaware that the ballyhoo was connected to the boat. The drop back in free spool is crucial. It conveys to the billfish the illusion that it has a free lunch, no strings attached.

Ballyhoo in jaw, the fish turned and ran. It streaked ten, fifteen, twenty yards, maintaining an even speed, line

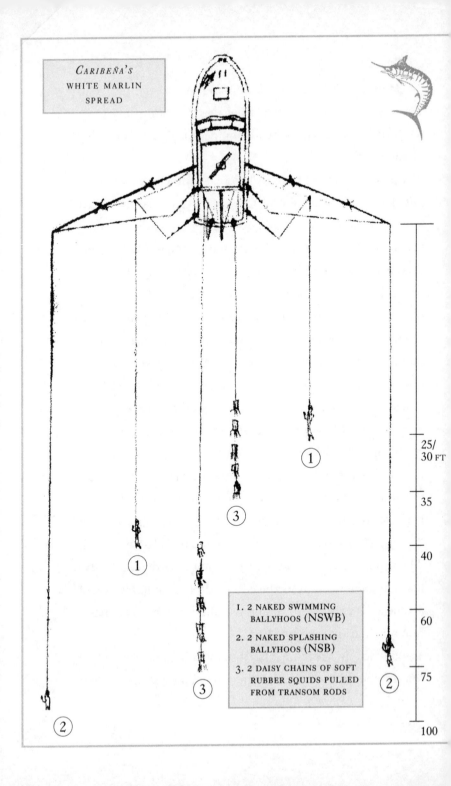

CARIBEÑA'S
WHITE MARLIN
SPREAD

25/
30 FT

35

40

60

75

100

1. 2 NAKED SWIMMING
   BALLYHOOS (NSWB)

2. 2 NAKED SPLASHING
   BALLYHOOS (NSB)

3. 2 DAISY CHAINS OF SOFT
   RUBBER SQUIDS PULLED
   FROM TRANSOM RODS

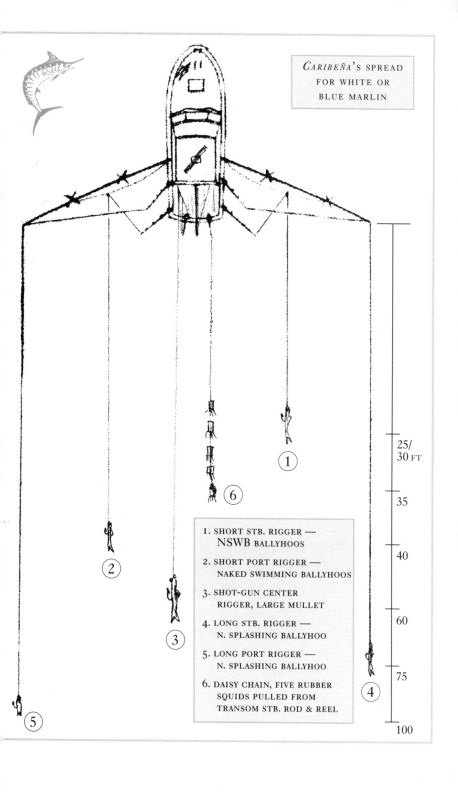

CARIBEÑA'S SPREAD
FOR WHITE OR
BLUE MARLIN

1

6

25/
30 FT

35

2

40

3

60

1. SHORT STB. RIGGER —
   NSWB BALLYHOOS

2. SHORT PORT RIGGER —
   NAKED SWIMMING BALLYHOOS

3. SHOT-GUN CENTER
   RIGGER, LARGE MULLET

4. LONG STB. RIGGER —
   N. SPLASHING BALLYHOO

5. LONG PORT RIGGER —
   N. SPLASHING BALLYHOO

6. DAISY CHAIN, FIVE RUBBER
   SQUIDS PULLED FROM
   TRANSOM STB. ROD & REEL

75

4

5

100

burning off the reel. Then came the pause, *the slight pause*, which I think is the instant that marlin use to accommodate the bait in their tongueless mouth, before accelerating again as if to use the flow of water to push the bait in and down, head first. I felt the pause through my thumb and heard a moment of hesitation in the diminished whine of reel. This is the instant to stop the free flow of line, or drop back, to pull up the reel's lever to engage the drag, and pause, briefly, until one feels the pull of the fish stretching the line. That's the time to strike.

One can read water, know the fish's habits, be a superb boatman, have well-rigged baits, but *consistently* catching white marlin—the most difficult of all species to hook— very often comes down to this one small pause, the fraction of a second, the hair's breadth, *el momento preciso*, in which intuition takes over, provoking an unhesitating reflex that caused me to flip the reel's lever, engage the drag, cut the flow of free line, and brace for the marlin's pull. One has to dig deep into the unconscious brain and wrest away from anxiety those extra seconds of patience, to yield and let the marlin take, take, take, and take even more line, until you "feel" in your thumb, in your heart, in your guts that *this* is the time to end the marlin's free ride. Intuitively you lock. Reflexively you strike.

The butt of my rod was firmly set in the cup, or pouch, of my small leather fighting belt, protecting both my stomach and manhood. Knees bent, legs apart, I repeatedly jerked the rod back against my right shoulder, one, two, three times—momentarily straightening my hunched shoulders and back—the force coming from my pumping forearms. My hook had pierced the white's bony mouth, the rod bowed, and the fish shot skyward, diving and jumping. Its seven-foot body flexed in the air, wrapped in a cascading curtain of glistening spray. It started its tail walk, fencing with the leader connected to the fishing line in an attempt to chafe it or shake the hook from its hold. But I gave it no slack. The fight was on.

Immediately after the aerial display, the fish sounded, stripping off two hundred yards of line. I maneuvered the boat with the cockpit controls, engaging the engines, one at a time, making sure none of my other lines crossed the one with the marlin. When the fish jumped beyond the farthest bait, I stopped the boat. Holding the rod with my left hand, I reeled in with the right, first the daisy chain, then the long starboard rigger line. With that side of the boat clear of lines, I was ready to pump my lucky rod, recoup some line, and bring the fish close to the boat for the final stage of our fight.

It wasn't that easy to lift the submerged fifty-plus-pound marlin with a twenty-pound test line. To back down the boat, I had to bring in the other two baits. Then I was ready to pursue the fish, which was tiring, coming up. Again it jumped, trying to throw the hook or break the line, but with only five pounds of drag, it didn't have a chance. Barely submerged, it ran fast to port, but like a rodeo horse accustomed to dealing with darting calves, *Caribeña* was fast on its tail. The white veered toward starboard and jumped; I backed down and reeled in, and soon the bimini knot and part of the black dacron trace touched the tip of the rod and were coiled into the reel's spool.

It was official. I had a catch. But I was not yet done. Armed with my tagging pole, I grabbed the six-foot-long leader and, with a quick move, inserted a tag on the marlin's shoulder. I pulled the fish even closer and, leaning over the gunwales, grabbed the white's long bill and looked into its open mouth; the regular "J" hook was in its lower jaw. The fish centered its eyes on the firm grip of my hand. Perhaps tired, or sensing good will on my part, it acted as if tamed.

With torso and head hanging out over the water, arms stretched, one hand on the beast's fearsome weapon, the other perilously close to the hook in its mouth, and the boat riding up and down on the swells, I had to be careful of my every move. I didn't want to have a hook embedded in my hand or be stabbed by the white's sword.

A stab wound inflicted by a marlin's sword could be lethal if the sword pierced my lungs or heart or slashed the carotid artery at the sides of my neck. It was all too easy to imagine what the outcome of such an accident would be. Being pulled overboard by the marlin was another potentially lethal situation with no one aboard to throw a life buoy, turn the boat around, or radio for help.

Finally, I forced the hook from the marlin's jaw. I pushed

its head down into the water, eased my grasp on its bill, and let the fish free. Unharmed and strong, the marlin extended his pectoral fins like a flying bird and glided along *Caribeña*'s port side for a second or two, and then the Prince of the Atlantic dove, embraced by the warm water of the Gulf Stream.

In the past, I have created concern among my friends and relatives when I've decided to stay overnight on the ocean. The first time that I didn't let anybody know I wouldn't return to port after a fishing day, *Caribeña*'s empty slip alarmed my neighbors, particularly John and Mary Sippel, whose boat, *Wire Nut*, was berthed to my port side. The night of my absence, John tried several times to raise me on the VHF only to find silence at the other end. He called Paul Daisey, a mutual friend, and was reassured to learn that the Coast Guard had not received a distress call. The Coast Guard may have tried to reach me, but they were bound to fail: I often have my radios turned off as they, if on, are incompatible with the most important aspect of my solitary overnight experiences—my solitude under a canopy of flickering stars.

I hadn't been completely out of touch, however. I had radioed *The Elixir* of my intention to stay overnight. Pat Kelly, *The Elixir*'s captain, volunteered to come by from twenty or thirty miles away at the end of their fishing day to drop off a case of butterfish—the classic overnight chunking bait.

Later, he had come back on the radio to ask about my present position. I had seen the white dot of his vessel advancing steadily toward the center of my radar screen. Finally, *The Elixir* appeared, reflecting sunlight like a low-flying comet, glowing and alive, leaving a white trail against the scumbled line of horizon and sky.

In a matter of minutes, the powerful boat drew a semicircle with its bow, passing a quarter of a mile off my port side. Pat slowed it to a stop, reversed, and smoothly backed *The Elixir*'s stern against my boat's bow where I stood with my thighs pressed against the rail. *Caribeña* barely drifted as Pat kept the vessels inches apart, a distance he immediately increased when the box of bait was in my hands, adding two or three feet between boats—theirs almost double the size of mine; its price tag, tenfold.

I briefly talked with Anthony "Tony" Williams, a residential developer, *The Elixir*'s owner, and Al Bednarik, a cohort of Tony's who was fishing with him that day. As with many sportfishing boats, the owner had hired a captain and crew. Both Tony and Al are accomplished and passionate sportfishermen, mature, serious Marylanders whom I have known since 1985 when the then-smaller *The Elixir*, a sportfishing Viking 35′, was docked on my starboard side at Mariner's Wharf, *Caribeña*'s Ocean City home. Tony told me they had caught and released a white marlin that day, missed another one, and raised a third that never struck. They also had caught four nice yellowfin tunas, all of similar size, in the seventy-pound class.

"You're staying overnight!" said Al.

"Yes," I said.

Tony shook his head. "Man, aren't you afraid to be alone, so far from port? I couldn't do that, even in daylight. I would be afraid to fish alone. Too many things can go wrong."

I know Al and Tony well. They are keen fishermen who have won their share of tournaments and battled many large fish, among them a 762-pound blue marlin. Its replica hangs on the wall in the Ocean City Marlin Clubhouse.

As we chatted, it felt as though we could well have been drinking a few beers in any bar at any street corner in any town in the world, but we were in fact sixty miles offshore. They stood in their cockpit, leaning against the wide gunwales of their impressive new boat, a heavyweight contender with twenty-four hundred horses corralled in the engine room, capable of surpassing forty knots. They were a short hour-and-a-half cruise from the Ocean City Inlet, a ride that would have taken me twice as long. They wished me luck and cruised off, and in minutes we were to one another's eyes shrinking marine stamps on opposing horizons. The last time I looked, the sun and *The Elixir* were a quivering mirage of orange and white, fast disappearing in their westerly race to twilight.

Minutes after I released my first white, a second marlin threw a hook during its aerial display, releasing himself without the protocol of a formal fight. A third marlin that showed up on my starboard long rigger line didn't like that particular bait, and swam up thirty feet just to check the short rigger bait. Still not convinced of the quality of that morsel, he went across *Caribeña*'s wake, like a dog chasing a car. This time he struck the ballyhoo closer to the boat on the port side. Two times I had run behind holding rods with rejected baits and then finally caught up with the finicky fish and was able to hook him up. Spectacular jumps preceded a long, deep run, but once I had him back on the surface jumping again, we had a short fight followed by a quick tag placement, and a clean release. Then, everything went calm again, validating my experience that white marlin seldom strike around sunset.

The sun fell behind a distant herd of clouds, hardly moving on a northeasterly course. Compact and corrugated, the clouds were woolly and looked like the grazing merino sheep I had observed in my youth. I thought of my mother and her love for sunsets and how she would have enjoyed the vast open ocean, the challenge of deep-sea fishing for marlin, the constantly changing sky, and this unique mantle of solitude adding wings to my thoughts.

In the remaining twilight, evanescent schools of skipping bait moved north, often chased and corralled by tuna, the huge predator at the tail of small prey, both airborne, the fifteen-inch fish unable to escape the fatal embrace of the tuna's powerful jaws.

I trolled with only two lines by the edge of an oily patch produced by the carnage of a school of feeding tunas. Busy in pursuit of the abundant live food, however, the tunas ignored my dead baits, and the marlin, if any were around, never showed up behind them.

A trailing breeze carried into *Caribeña*'s cockpit and my nostrils the strong, fishy smell of the bait's freshly ripped flesh. Pulling only two lines, I was avoiding having to contend with four simultaneous tuna bites at dusk. It may sound strange to a meat fisherman, but although I may be fishing, I don't necessarily want to catch tuna. Not at this particular time. I would like to hook up with another marlin, a white marlin, but not a blue, that is, if the gods changing guard at the very edge of day and night would allow me to choose with whom to fight.

I deemed that a blind match with a white in the twilight would take a maximum of fifteen minutes to bring to an end, but to fight a large blue in the dark of the night, as I remember well, can take forever, probably consuming all the hours I wanted to devote to the swordfish, the Lord of the Abyss, Emperor of the Night.

With no wind, waves, or moon, the night ocean was silent and black. I kept seeing a dim white light popping up at erratic intervals on top of faraway swells. A long-liner, I thought, coming back to the head of its set. While I don't mind fishing in close quarters during the day, at night I want to keep a distance of three or four miles with any other boats. Because of the tall swells, that night I made my mind to position myself five or six miles away from where I knew the long-liners to be. That would be enough for safety and would provide adequate room for them to work.

It was now after nine, and there I was, *disfrutando la noche*, enjoying my break, enjoying the pause, all fishing suspended, comfortably seated on a chair on the deck of my drifting boat, forcing my body to rest for the first time since the early dawn.

I propped up my feet, holding a cold drink in my warm hand, feeling a cooling breeze from the southwest. Between sips, I watched the hypnotic rise and fall of gigantic swells, the rippling effect produced by the northbound hurricane, still hundreds of miles from these coasts.

I thought of the devastating damage done by such cyclones. Then the ebony sky glowed in the east, and soon a bright moon rose on the horizon as if jumping rope with the curving swells.

I had the best seat in the house, and I was loath to relinquish it. Only for food did I suspend my contemplation, and for not more than two or three jumps of the moon. Ensconced back in my chair with a big aromatic bowl of mahi-mahi seviche, I couldn't have been more content.

Grateful for my day, I let my thoughts wander: that morning I had left the dock at 4:00 A.M., cruising out into the ocean, following *Las Tres Marias* until sunrise, those three stars imperfectly aligned in the belt of Orion that I have been noticing since I was a child. Then I followed my hunch and instincts until sunset. The celestial display and the fishing success had made my day—but the journey was not yet complete. A whole night lay ahead for boat and mind to drift.

Seventy-two miles offshore, drifting north by northeast at two-and-half knots over an average depth of 3,000 feet, I felt as if I were at the top of the world.

After dinner, I thought of fishing just one line. I turned on two floodlights to illuminate *Caribeña*'s cockpit where I rigged a pair of baits. With a short stainless-steel needle and a long waxed thread, I sowed my hooks under the skirts of some squid, preparing dinner for a mighty swordfish. But the truth is, I am not a serious fisherman at night. At night, I am more interested in the secrets of the universe and the twists of life than in the rewards of a catch. The bounty I chase has little to do with fins and scales. I would like to compare endurance and strength with this fish that can reach 500-plus pounds in this part of the Atlantic, but, if we fight and I win, I would not kill the fish. Long-liners do. Every day. And every night. With my one hook, the chances of finding a swordfish eager to eat my bait are almost nil compared to the commercial fleet.

Books like *The Perfect Storm* and *The Hungry Ocean* have made a romance out of commercial fishing. Their protagonists, like all other long-liner fishermen, including *Hungry Ocean* author *Swordboat* Captain Linda Greenlaw, all fish for a living; mercenaries at sea, they roam the oceans to enrich their bank accounts. Perhaps they love the sea; but I, for one (and I suspect I speak for the other fifty million sport fisher-men in the United States), see neither glamour nor skill in killing a thousand swordfish and scores of other fish caught on each line's undiscriminating 4,000 hooks.

At the very least, it's a different kind of glamour and skill from my crew of one, the old gray beard trolling at most five baits. I, too, live to fish—as much as any long-liner. Offshore is also my home. But it is solitude on the sea that awakens my soul and quickens my spirit. The challenge of the sport is my goal. At the end of my hunt, I have no trophy fish to show for my effort. I have something better. What I haul back to the dock I can keep in my heart and mind. And, in my book, that's what counts.

I sat back in my chair on *Caribeña*'s deck and looked up at the stars, fishing through the oceans of my mind. I heard the soft slap of water in the port chine. Blended with lim-ited stripes and splashes of moonlight, the ocean's shadows stretched away from me on all sides, vast and black. I looked up at the stars and thought of Carl Sagan, who wrote in *Cosmos*:

One full molecule of human DNA has about a hundred mil-lion such twists and about a hundred billion atoms, as many as the number of stars in a typical galaxy.

Since there are some hundred billion galaxies in the uni-verse, it shouldn't sound irreverent if I say that, perhaps, we are not at the shores of the cosmic ocean but only on the shores of a tiny cosmic creek. Physicists now theorize that our whole known universe, those 12 or 15 billion light-years of galaxies upon galaxies across the space, very well may be only one among hundreds of billions of similarly vast universes—themselves, in the spatial scheme, nothing more than a single molecule of water lost in the middle of the Pacific Ocean. Some scientists, like Andrei Linde of Stanford University, have started to embrace the hypothesis that the universe is constantly re-creating itself, giving birth to new universes. It's mind-blowing to think that all of this is happening beyond our local universe. This is Eternity itself. I think if there were a God and God blinked in our allotted "cosmic time" in Eternity, God would miss the birth, life, and death of our own sun and its planetary entourage, for in the infinite scale of Eternity, the presumed 10 billion years of the sun's life span would have been a nanosecond flash or, to be more accurate, in Eternal terms, a nonevent.

No wonder I feel that each second of life counts. We don't have much time in our brief existence. Is this life the whole journey? Or is it a mere passage? A way station, perhaps? Looking at the stars on this night, I was sure that it is the evolving present that matters.

My diminishing allotment of years has made me ask the eternal questions: Who are we? Where are we? But, on this night, I was saved from further philosophizing by the proverbial bell.

A loud nocturnal bite brought me back to the here and

now. Line whined off the reel. I grabbed my rod, and struck, and the fish exploded in a run of forty miles per hour, or more. The tip of the rod remained glued to the air while the rest of the upper pole formed an arc. "Big fish," I thought, seeing the line fly out of the spool at such a speed. In thirty seconds, I had lost almost all of my 500 yards. Fortunately, fishing only one line, I immediately backed down my boat, and the fish slowed down and sounded, which made me think tuna rather than swordfish. Tuna fishing doesn't require a special skill or degree of finesse. It's a tug-of-war. A battle of muscles.

"Definitely yellowfin," I said aloud. "Seventy or eighty pounds, at least." And puffing, "One hundred, perhaps." I knew I would have to fight for a while. "A while" in the dark seemed much longer than the thirty-some minutes that took me to bring back the eighty-pound tuna close to the boat. She was circling counterclockwise, instinctually keeping herself at a safe distance from the unfriendly gaff—but the battle of wills was winding down. Leader in hand with a cautious single wrap (I would hate to be pulled overboard anytime, but particularly at night), I planted the gaff next to the gill plate and pushed up at the same time, lifting the yellowfin over the gunwales. Reluctantly she came aboard. She didn't fit in my fish box. I was forced to leave her over the deck, covered with bags of ice, making deep cuts on the top of her head, under the lateral fin and round her tail—the first in a sequence of steps to optimize the quality of her meat.

After my tuna battle, I finally paid attention to the repeated hints of my tiring body: soon I would have to rest. I
rebaited my hook and lowered it into the black water. Then
I went to the fly bridge and made sure that the radar alarm
was on, ready to alert me if anything came within three
miles of my boat. The long-liners were five miles away.
Changing the radar scales, I scanned the surrounding ocean
up to twelve miles around *Caribeña*; only a large dot popped
up on the screen's edge. A freighter or a long-liner, eleven
miles away and invisible to the naked eye. My white anchor
light was on, visible all around for at least two miles. I
checked my drift. I was being pushed north, which meant
the two long-liners at work would remain to my south, the
distance between us probably increasing during the night.

With all the plastic curtains rolled up in *Caribeña*'s fly
bridge, I felt the breeze, filling my lungs with the salty smell
of the sea. It was coming more from the south than the
southwest. I checked again the freighter's position; now
twelve miles away, moving on a southerly course, ready to
fall off from the edge of the radar screen and my brief list of
concerns. I went down and checked the reel's drag one more
time. Fine. The click was on. I would hear its screeching cry
if a fish were to pick up and move away with my bait. The
engines were quiet, much quieter than in any other boat I
have ever fished, partly good engine-room insulation, partly
the engines themselves, and mostly because after all these
years I don't hear them anymore. I mean, not in an intrusive

manner. I'm accustomed to their humming—which I per-
ceive as *Caribeña*'s mantra reverberating at sea. I threw a
cover over the salon's floor and a pillow on top. Finally, I lay
down, head to bow, legs to stern, feet with shoes by the
opening to the cockpit, the reel reachable with a single jump.

It was now well past midnight. On my overnights, I cat-
nap; my sleep is never deep. During the early morning hours,
I stood up and walked outside three, four, maybe five times
and noted that the line in the reel hadn't moved. Bunches of
loose sargasso weed passed by the stern, and I could see several squids darting by and three or four small groups of look-
alike needlefish. I reeled in my bait and checked it. Some
small fish had been nibbling at it; the tubular skirt of the
squid was partially gone. I put on a fresh bait and lowered it
again, this time to 120 feet, just above the thermocline line.
That was my last try for swordfish that night.

Soon, the long-liners were gone. Pale and low, the moon
appeared determined to avoid daylight. I lay down over the
fish box and faced the skies. It was humbling to observe the
night dissolve itself into a blushing dawn. Finally, at sunrise,
I engaged *Caribeña*'s engines, put my lines into the water,
and became a serious angler again.

T W O

·

·

A CREW OF ONE

The beach resort of Ocean City, Maryland, where I returned with *Caribeña*, is home for 10,000 local residents who live year-round in this narrow beach town. But at the height of summer, the population balloons to more than 300,000 people who come to swim, sunbathe, snorkel, water-ski, parasail, golf, eat, shop, dance, ride the Ferris wheel, stroll the three-mile boardwalk . . . and, of course, to fish.

At twenty-two knots, my reentry into civilization took almost four hours. I was ready to relax, have a good hot meal, and get a comfortable night of sleep on my regular bed. Unlike most other captains and mates who can afford taking turns on their boats, I can't sleep coming back home: I have to be constantly on the lookout for other boats or whatever else might be in our path: buoys, sleepers (partially submerged logs), jetsam that didn't sink, and the common flotsam found at sea.

I sat comfortably on the cushioned long bench in front of *Caribeña*'s bridge controls. The bridge is a perfect place to observe and unwind, and while relaxing there, I mulled over the marlin's behavior that in the rush of action hadn't registered in its full depth and detail. I caressed in mind the savage intent of the first white's bill trying to chafe the leader—and the second white's miss of the bait in its initial angry surge, so determined to eat on its successful comeback. I also thought of Ocean City's upcoming White Marlin Open Tournament. The mere idea of the competition to come brought a rush of anticipation and excitement. From now on, all my thoughts and actions in this particular vein would be closely related to *the* contest.

Ocean City bills itself as "The White Marlin Capital of the World." And every August, the town capitalizes on its white marlin capital status by hosting one of the premier events in all of angling, the annual White Marlin Open Tournament—the WMOT, the most prominent and prestigious marlin-fishing competition in the Atlantic, possibly in the world. For a week, deep-sea anglers from far and wide converge on the back bays of the little town on a Maryland sandbar. They come from countries like Australia and Bermuda, and locally, they come from as far south and west as Texas and California and as far north as New York and Maine; they hail from innumerable ports and inlets along the East Coast and some from the Gulf Coast. They include veterans as well as rookies, world-class fishing teams with professional crews, weekend warriors, the skilled, the lucky, the shrewd, the ordinary, men and women from all walks of life. They come to try their luck and test their skills as they attempt to catch the biggest marlin and, if they can, the most marlin, and carry home the money—and the prestige—that are the prizes of the White Marlin Open.

The Open began as pretty much a local affair: at its 1974 inauguration, only fifty-two boats registered. I first entered the Open five years later, in 1979, with my first boat, and I participated sporadically until 1985, the first year I owned *Caribeña*. Since then, the WMOT and I have grown older to- gether, and we've both grown in girth as well, till today— indeed, since the late 1980s—the Open is recognized as the world's largest billfish tournament.

The storm that had threatened to come in the previous night had by morning changed its course and had blown it- self out to sea. The swells were now half their nocturnal size, and close to coast, the seas had become flat. Ten miles off the inlet of Ocean City, I could see the emerging silhou- ettes of twenty-story buildings that rise up on the north beach. Soon, I also saw the two towering city water tanks and the Ferris wheel at the south end of town.

Not many boats were around. But in seven days, the tour- nament would create coastal rush hours early in the mornings and late in the afternoons. As Ocean City's busy board-walk gained definition, I reviewed the bait I'd need for the tournament. Ake Marine would provide a case with a dozen of twelve-pack medium-sized ballyhoos and medium-sized mullets. Delmarva Sport Center would supply large, black mullets, twenty-inch Spanish mackerels, and perhaps a pair of big, bulky squids. Huge baits for the huge blue. And I would drop by Skip's Bait and Tackle Shop to say hi to the old man and buy his large horse ballyhoos—the best in town.

At Ake's, they will inspect and service my *big guns* for the big blue marlin, the two Penn International reels called "50 wide," replacing the old line with new eighty-pound test. I'd take care of the small reels, "15's" and "20's" Shimanno, and the "12's" and "20's" Penn International, all suitable for white marlin, though borderline for big tunas and questionable for a large bigeye. I will use Tournament Ande lines, for always they test right, and in a game so full of uncertainties, at least I would know the real strength of my lines. Bill Gordy, the diver, will replace *Caribeña*'s current pair of propellers with newly polished ones. I'm convinced that shiny blades gather and reflect more light under troll, attract fish, and add an extra edge to my marlin search.

I wondered how many boats would enter the tournament. The previous year there had been over two hundred. In the fishing community, among my peers (anglers, boat owners, and crew), the prestige of winning the White Marlin Open is immense—not to mention the tournament's financial rewards. We will vie against one another for nearly $1 million in prizes.

The official prizes in 1995 reached a total of $790,420. The heaviest white marlin, at 69 pounds, caught by Rod Rippin aboard the North Carolinian *Temptress,* with Captain Chip Shafer, earned $193,007. However, Pete Donnelly's smaller 68-pound white caught aboard the *Sea Hag*—that unlike the *Temptress* had entered in all the betting categories—collected prizes totaling $286,253. Warren Halle, of Potomac, Maryland, took home $179,757 for his 522-pound blue marlin. The rest of the monetary prizes were distributed among the other anglers who caught the heaviest pelagics during the week.

Part of this money comes from the entrance fee of $750 paid by each participant boat. The rest comes from the official calcuttas, formed by five tiers of betting or skill levels: $300, $700, $1,000, $2,000, and $5,000. Some teams, thinking they can win big money, enter their vessels across the board, contributing to the general fund a maximum of $9,750, not an insubstantial amount to bet on one fish. In addition, there may be unofficial dockside bets where untold amounts of cash are discreetly handed over in brown paper bags.

But for many of us, the possibility of a financial windfall is not as important as the chance to win the plaque for Best Boat, a Master Ring for the Best Angler, the honor of being named the Captain of the Year or Mate of the Year, titles that also warrant commemorative Master Rings and brand their recipients as the best of the best.

These are the tournament's emotional rewards—and the inestimable worth that one can assign to a genuine batch of firm, friendly handshakes and to the congratulatory pats on the back, or even to the occasional kiss from the woman pressing your hard, muscled fishing arm as she tells you how much she admires you for being part of the Open and for going far offshore after the big game of the sea.

With three miles to go until I reached Ocean City—exactly nine minutes at twenty knots—I judged it safe to go down to the cockpit and attached two inverted white marlin flag to the right rigger halyard line (the inverted flags signifying that I had released the fish). On purpose I delayed hoisting them, allowing my boat's structure to partially shield the flags, not from true wind—for there was none—but from the strong rushing draft created by *Caribeña*'s run, which could tear the flags apart or blow them into the sea.

With half the ritual completed, I returned to the bridge, only hoisting the flags when I had nearly reached the sentinel pair of buoys that indicates the safest entrance to the inlet. The brackish waters of the back bays rushed with their ebbing tides to embrace *Caribeña*'s hull. The fluttering applause of my flags symbolized our success.

There were friendly smiles and thumbs up as Harbor Island welcomed *Caribeña* back into her birth. I tied up and then cut the engines and, still on the fly bridge, heard the customary questions shouted from the dock. Where had I caught the fish? What was the weather offshore? A small crowd around me wanted to know if I had caught something else besides the two marlin announced by my flags. I mentioned my mahimahi-seviche dinner; the onlookers shook their heads, some approvingly, some not sure what to think of a raw repast.

"Did you see anything else?" one woman asked.

"A gorgeous moonrise, gigantic swells, a starry night." Close to dinnertime, most didn't want to hear my reveries. They were after something they could cook and eat! They wanted fish!

I smiled, and became deliberately slow with words. ". . . a most beautiful night . . ."

They started to thin out. "Then, no other bites?" said *mi amigo* Ernesto in a disappointed tone.

I answered his question with one of my own. "I bet you would have wanted to clean the fish if I caught one, wouldn't you?"

"It would have been a pleasure."

And I knew that for a fact. An avid fisherman himself, this affable Argentinian-Cuban neighbor had proved himself a noble man.

"I did have a bite. A tuna bite." I had his full attention.

"How big?"

"I don't know," said I, turning and picking up my short hand gaff. "It felt big!" With the hook and my remaining strength, I lifted the yellowfin tuna I had behind the fishing box, thinking that it was at least eighty pounds.

"What you think?"

"A Yellowfin!" said my surprised friend.

"*Atún de Aleta Amarilla.*" I put the tuna on the dock. "Let me get you my filleting knife. I do appreciate your offer to clean the fish."

He stepped down and jumped into my boat.

"Here you are. You can take home as much tuna as you want."

"*Muchas gracias!*" He took the sheathed knife and the sharpening stone in one hand while shaking my hand with the other.

I agreed to meet Ernesto at the fish-cleaning station on Harbour Island to weigh my tuna and then share a beer. After taking a shower on board *Caribeña*, I changed clothes and drove to the weighing station. There I found Ernesto and the tuna, which was roped by its tail and ready to hoist. The scale registered eighty-six pounds. Afterward, it didn't take long for Ernesto to dress the fish and bag dozens of fresh red steaks. The lingering dusk of midsummer had descended over the wharf. Done with the fish, we walked with a couple of friends the fifty yards separating the weight station from the Reel Inn Grille. The firm, motionless concrete felt strange under my legs, so accustomed was I after my overnight to *Caribeña*'s pitch and swing. Seated at the bar, drink in hand, raising my voice over Bob Marley's hypnotic beat, I ordered whatever they had ready on the grill. Coincidentally, it was yellowfin tuna.

The first thing I did when the grilled fish was presented

to me over a bed of romaine was to inhale the superb aroma of this gift from the sea, impregnating my senses with the dish's mix of fresh greens, vinegar, and freshly ground peppercorn. From the first bite, there was no doubt: it was indeed a real catch of the day, and the meat and its taste were what I was hoping for. It was seared outside, with a firm, deliciously marinated browned crust, which perfectly balanced its pink and tender inside.

After his beer, Ernesto took off with several bags of yellowfin tuna steaks to *Caribeña*, and some more bags that he would bring home. Over coffee, I conversed with Jonathan Duffie, owner of the *Billfisher*; Ron Hoffman, of the *Sea Roamer*; and Gary Lilly, from the *Dixie Lady*, all members of the Ocean City Marlin Club. The subject: marlin fishing. The focus: the Open. The question: Would we be able to find marlin during that week?

We speculated for a while. Finally we said good-bye on the dock in the dark of night. We'd see one another next week—here, and probably offshore as well. I drove back to Mariner's Wharf and before my much-needed and well-earned good night's sleep, I stopped by the boat. Thanks to Skip Daisey, who had come by while I was having dinner, *Caribeña* was immaculately clean. Rods and reels—washed and dried—were back each in their places; my tackle stored away. Ernesto had left several plastic zip bags containing red tuna steaks covered by ice inside the small cooler on the cockpit. I didn't see the yellowfin's head, so I assumed it was in the crab pot of a teenager who docked his boat two slips down the dock and had asked for it. I may end up tasting a few crabs from his crop. Sharing the fruits of the sea fortifies the backbone of friendship.

I slept in the condo I used to keep in Ocean City before driving back early the next day to my home in Annapolis. The condo was a two-bedroom apartment on the third story with a large balcony overlooking the Harbor Island Marina where the registration for the tournament would be held the following weekend. *Caribeña* was moored in front of the condo and right across from the Reel Inn Grille.

From Annapolis, I would drive the hour it would take to get to several prearranged meetings with the managers and chefs of my restaurants in and around Washington, D.C. At that point, I had three El Caribe: the original, opened in 1974, was at 1828 Columbia Road, N.W., in the heart of *el barrio Latino*, in Adams Morgan; the second came in 1977 in the quaint and fashionable Georgetown; and the third, at 8130 Wisconsin Avenue, was in Bethesda, where restaurants used to be few and never more than one or two per city block, but that was in 1985. The three El Caribe had basically the same menu, all serving Spanish and Latin-American fare; a fourth, Candelas, opened in 1980, specialized in northern Italian food, and was next door to El Caribe of Georgetown, both connected inside through an arched opening made in the century-old, two-feet-thick stone wall that divided the historic buildings. I also had a fifth restaurant, called La Posada, in Bethesda, a popular Mexican/Tex-Mex, with its entrance on Woodmont Avenue (parallel to Wisconsin Avenue). La Posada was back to back to El Caribe on the same city block, the two establishments connected by a central kitchen, and, in that sense, these places were like Siamese culinary twins.

If, twenty years before, the map of my life had a path leading to my future restaurants, I did not notice it—not until I was standing in front of a fork in the road. One road of this bifurcation was well known, paved with security and easy to stroll, but it seemed to me rather plain. The other branch, behind the neon and glamour, hinted a mix of hard work and rewards at the end of what I was told could be rougher than a roller-coaster ride. But I felt confident. I made my choice and became a restaurateur.

Being a radio and TV announcer in Montevideo connected me with advertising agencies and with the radio Section of USIS (United States Information Service) in Uruguay, where I learned about Voice of America broadcasting in Spanish to Latin America, which was in part what eventually brought me to the United States. That was the dream of my first wife, then a librarian with La Biblioteca Nacional in Uruguay.

In 1969, at age twenty-eight, with more than ten years of experience as a broadcaster—after passing writing, translating, and voicing tests—I was hired by Voice of America (its studios housed in the old HEW Building with the now-defunct Department of Health, Education and Welfare in southwest Washington, D.C.). Soon after, I competed for and won a newscaster position with the Mutual Broadcasting System (then with its studios in the National Press Building on 14th Street). As a member of AFTRA (American Federation of Television and Radio Artists), I was ensured very good pay for writing and voicing three daily newscasts in the morning hours, directed to more than eighty Spanish radio stations in the States. I saved my money, and without any background other than being accustomed to eating well, and lured by the perceived independency of working for myself and the enormous challenge of coming into a business where it was difficult to succeed, I bought my first restaurant in 1974.

The first thing I did was hire a good chef. I didn't know that he had a notorious bad temper and that his professional talent and energy were fueled by his furtive drinking of alcohol. He had worked before in the kitchen of the English Embassy, and later in a Spanish restaurant co-owned by an Irish-American man. When this restaurateur learned that I was hiring his former chef, he betted me that—given my personality and the track record of his ex-chef—I would fire him in less than six months if not in a much shorter time, or, if forced to work dry, the newly hired chef would soon resign. One or the other, his tenure would be brief. I disagreed, and we bet a deep-sea fishing trip out of Ocean City, with the losing party to pay the charter-boat bill.

Once at work, from the very beginning I noticed that

several bottles, and particularly the Chivas Regal bottle, were under attack. The bar door's being locked during the day did not prevent the morning chef's assault. After changing locks, the bottled wines in the dining room came under siege, and, later, the cooking wine in the kitchen. Adding salt to the cooking wine brewed contempt and, at other times, sincere promises of abstinence, with the occasional relapse . . . but the chef stayed for six months. I won the free fishing trip, caught a white marlin, and during the next fifteen years—with the same chef on the payroll until his untimely death—we went on to win twelve Blue Ribbon Awards given to the best ten restaurants in town by the food editors of the popular *Washingtonian* magazine.

But not everything went well. While winning commercial accolades, I was accumulating painful losses in my personal life. First, in 1980, I lost my father-in-law, and soon after, my first marriage, already weak, collapsed and ended in divorce. Sadly, my teenage daughter sided with her mom, and rarely have we spoken since. In 1983, I suddenly lost my mother, only one week after I had returned from a wonderful three-week visit with her in Uruguay. Two years later, my father became very sick. I drove from North Carolina back to D.C., and from there I flew overnight to Uruguay. He had repeatedly been asking for me. I was anxious to arrive; he, ready to leave, waited for one last hug. It was the last time I was in Uruguay. At forty-four, I found myself truly alone in this world.

That year, I stopped expanding my business. I knew then that I would eventually sell my restaurants and somehow go back to my roots and perhaps write a book or two. In Spanish, I thought.

But in the mid-1990s, still heavily involved in these restaurants, my managers and chefs would have to run the places without me for a few days during the tournament.

That week in Annapolis, I ate well, drank my favorite drink, a single peach margarita concocted with my ultra-secret recipe, got plenty of sleep, and kept myself in good physical shape. Then I packed up my car and headed back to Ocean City, 100 miles beyond the curving spans of the four-and-a-half-mile-long bridge over the Chesapeake Bay.

On this drive, I always stop in the heart of commercial Easton, at the castle of my sweet darling: The Dairy Queen. I got attached years ago, and what a commitment it has been! A lifetime affair. I love her ice cream on the sugar cone, after it has been dipped in a dark, hot chocolate fudge. The good thing about this liaison is that it breaks the trip—half way to Ocean City I think of visiting her, and the other half goes fast, savoring the sweetness of our encounter, a date that never fails.

As I rolled into the city, I noticed that the waterfront sections of town had undergone a transformation in the week I'd been gone. The private docks and commercial marinas were now chock-full of some of the finest sportfishing boats in the world. Counting boat and equipment, many of their owners had invested anywhere from a half million to $3 million in their vessels. The local restaurants and tackle shops were full of boat owners, their families, fishermen, and among them the elite professional captains and mates, dedicated seamen, the very best that money could buy—their annual salaries and perks ranging from $60,000 to $100,000, or more.

This was not my first tournament. I had competed, in one way or another, as a marlin angler in my own boat for the last twenty years. Most years my odds of winning the tournament are slim against this army of bigger and faster boats with experienced crews and their most modern arsenals for catching fish. However, if marlin are scarce and scattered, the hunt would be tough for all. If few marlin rise to the baits, everyone has to capitalize on every chance strike. If this were the case, individual angler skills would become more important than the boat used in the hunt of billfish, and, de facto, my slim odds of winning would dramatically increase.

I had become involved in the tournament before I was invited to join the exclusive Ocean City Light Tackle Club (OCLTC) in 1980. Despite my solitariness as an angler, the club's invitation was one I felt I could not decline: the benefits of membership—in terms of comparing techniques, assistance, camaraderie, and cultivating long-lasting friendships—have been invaluable. But as busy as I was and as private as I've always been, I held off joining the Ocean City Marlin Club (OCMC), an older club with a much larger membership, until 1987 when I thought that my solitary fishing—

47

after ten years—was perhaps finally understood. During the seasons of 1985 and 1986, only 176 and 174 white marlin were caught by the whole fleet. Those same years, I had caught 11 and 10 from my own boat, but, not being a member, my marlin were not included in the official report. Given my luck on the lean years, the members of the board invited me to join for a second time, and I accepted. Since then, my billfish have counted in tallies made of the number of billfish caught and released off Ocean City.

The rules of OCMC membership require all members to report their marlin catch throughout the fishing season— important for tracking statistics on the species' viability. Another objective of this practice is to collect individual results and reward the small group of anglers who excel. At season's end, the club invites everyone to participate in an annual dinner where its directors present awards to its members for Top Boat of the Year, Top Angler, Most Marlin Released, Most Marlin Tagged, and so on. By joining the club, therefore, *Caribeña* and I automatically entered into this year-long competition with other members and boats.

I like the healthy competition of the club, which includes the week of the Open. I believe that among the many primeval instincts embedded deep in our genetic makeup is the instinct to test your skills and virtues against the skills and virtues of others, to strive constantly for betterment. We human beings keep competing against one another as we have done since the dawn of humankind, and competing is part of being.

Among sportfishermen, to be sure, the competitive instinct coexists with camaraderie—and necessarily so, for at sea, a sudden change in weather, a sudden mechanical failure, or a sudden misstep can put one's life on the line. At sea, a man can quickly become dependent on others for survival, and so the law of the sea predisposes all of us to lend a hand to any crew or boat in distress.

Proofs abound. Like anybody else going often to sea, I have had my share of mechanical breakdowns. After a fishing day, when I intended to return to port, one engine didn't respond. I couldn't restart it. I put my problem on the air, and fast came back the radioed suggestions from other boats in the area. The unanimous diagnosis was fuel contamination. I had to try this and I had to try that. In the end, the problem couldn't be fixed. I returned to Ocean City with only one engine running. At eight knots, it took me eight hours. But before losing radio contact with the fleet already under way, there came the final advice from Brad Watkins aboard his *Agitator:* "Carlos, even when the engine is shut off, the propeller turns. Put a wrench around the shaft to stop it from rotating; otherwise you could damage your transmission." I took the advice. Once I arrived to port after midnight, the problem—an air bubble in the fuel line—was quickly fixed, and I was able to fish the next day. But if Brad had not shared his knowledge, the collateral damage could have been a thousand times worse.

On another occasion, I arrived at the scene of what easily could have been a disaster that involved loss of life. On a serene, overcast morning devoid of wind, on the horizon off my port bow, I saw a plume of black smoke. Strange at sea, I thought. The anomaly alone told me something was wrong, and I altered course, ready to assist. At three miles away, I saw flames engulfing a vessel. Another boat was already racing toward the scene. Arriving, I saw only a charred flat mass above the waterline. Not even a transom. No name. Just a pit of fire and gutted hull. Avoiding the heavy smoke, I backed down *Caribeña* and picked up several items that had been tossed overboard and two empty orange life vests drifting away from the raging inferno.

"Is everybody on board?" I shouted over the engines to the other boat, *Par Five*, which had arrived first and had rescued the crew, who had abandoned ship.

"Yes, we have them all."

"Anything I can do?"

They waved "no thanks" with their hands.

Par Five ended up with fifteen people on board: eight of their own and seven from *The Sea Skill*, all surprised and scared.

This deep knowledge that we are all potentially dependent on one another brings a sense of brotherhood to the sport of fishing, which may be why so much of the activity of the weekend preceding the Open consists of meeting and greeting friends old and new.

The center of the action is a flock of tents erected on the waterfront of Harbor Island Marina, on the eastern shore of the Isle of Wight Bay, at the end of 14th Street. This is headquarters, the place where the Open participants register—a lively hub of conversation, shop talk, and catching up since last year's tournament. Memorabilia and jewelry stands have their clientele, and so does the bar of the Reel Inn Grille with its several outposts.

The weekend before the tournament, I crossed the eighty-yard-wide boat basin aboard the center console (a small open boat) that offered me a lift. By water, the trip took less than thirty seconds—that's how far the tents, the official scale, and the Reel Inn Grille are from my dock. Once *en tierra firme*, I walked through the crowds. Literally thousands of people had converged, carpeting the waterfront. Not only the participants but also their spouses, kids, family members, and significant others and friends were drawn to the event, as if by a magnet.

I picked my way through these throngs of curious onlookers who fill out the scene. They are drawn by the excitement, the carnival atmosphere, the shimmer and polish of some of the best sportfishing boats anywhere.

On the water around the registration area, and in marinas around town, all these vessels form part of this once-a-year formidable fleet. With their varied lengths, spotless, sparkling, the boats seem to radiate flashes of light as they bob on the water, skipping as far as their tethers will allow. Many of the boats arriving for the Open are part of a nomad group, a kind of gypsy fleet that follows the international route of migratory fish, creating a year-round season. Instead of wintering exclusively in Florida ports and waiting for summer back up north, as most fisher folks do, the members of the gypsy fleet head for waters with a sea surface temperature above the seventy-five-degree mark, the temperature at which the oceans and currents are warm enough to hold schools of bait. And where the bait goes, migratory billfish follow.

In America's autumn and early winter, you'll find the gypsy fleet in the Caribbean or off Caracas, Venezuela. By February, they may be as far south as Belize or as far west as the Gulf waters off Mexico—Cancún, Puerto Aventuras, Isla Mujeres, or Cozumel. Then, in the second half of May, they all make a U-turn—bait, fish, and behind them, boats and men, all coming back to the waters off the east coast of the United States. You can find these big boys from the gypsy fleet docking together at Singer Island in West Palm Beach or Fort Pierce just up the Florida coast; or at Morehead City, South Carolina; or in Pirate's Cove or the Fishing Center in Nags Head on North Carolina's Outer Banks; or in Cape May, New Jersey; or here in Ocean City—always in pursuit of the migratory billfish.

Thanks to these year-round wanderings, these captains and mates now speak a fair bit of Spanish, much to my delight. And they have mastered that indispensable fisherman's word—*nada*, "nothing," a word that is especially useful in the latitudes around Ocean City when you are reporting about marlin. After a few weeks back from Cancún or Caracas, they can say *nada* with no accent at all.

They are here in Ocean City now—the nomadic fleet with their world-class crews ready to compete among themselves, against their less globetrotting peers who may venture only as far as Hatteras or Cape May, and also against the comparatively sedentary local charter and private fleets, including the avocational boats like my *Caribeña*, the only boat with a crew of one—the only one, as far as I know, without a fighting chair.

As indispensable as fighting chairs seem to be for epic battles with large fish, I derive extra pleasure from fighting all my blue marlin just standing up. Many have been in the 300- to 500-pound range, and at least one has been as large as 700 pounds. Captain Robbie Paquette was a guest on my boat when I fought a blue, standing, for eight hours. Of course, a chair is a big help, but then it could be too much of an advantage for the angler working with a seat harness and the benefit of a footrest. I like the challenge of a more even competition. And I am willing to explore the limits of my physical endurance, so a fighting chair has no chance on my boat.

SUNDAY, AUGUST 4, 1996

As I strolled the docks on registration day, I felt that my week off in Annapolis had served me well. I returned with enough strength to fight for hours if necessary whatever dared to bite my bait. Two days of rest are mandatory in the

53

tournament and almost always needed—because of foul weather, mechanical problems, or physical exhaustion, probably in that order. The tournament's three grueling days of fishing offshore can be a test for both boats and men.

The tournament starts at 5:30 A.M.: no boat can go beyond the sea buoy laying outside Ocean City before that time. Fishing starts at 8:30 A.M. each day and ends at 3:30 P.M. The minimum weight of a white marlin that will "count" for the tournament's money prizes is 65 pounds. For blue marlin, the minimum is 300 pounds; 40 pounds for tuna; 20 pounds for wahoo and mahimahi; and 100 pounds for sharks. Anglers going for the monetary prizes, which are given for the biggest fish in several categories, must boat their catch for weighing back at the pier. Anglers going for the prestige prize, given for the most fish "caught," receive seventy points for each white marlin released but gain an extra five points if they can tag the fish; they report their catches by radio to the committee boat just after releasing the fish.

In the registration tent, the line was so long that I decided to wait to enter myself and *Caribeña* until later that day. My time would be better spent preparing tackle and baits. Always a stickler for detail, at tournament time I make extra sure everything is in place. Competing in offshore big-game fishing is just like going offshore big-game fishing for pleasure and recreation—only more intense. The idiosyncrasies of the sport take on a special edge; the demands seem more rigorous. The details you stopped think-

54

ing about long ago, if you've been fishing as long as I have, take on fresh meaning. You want to leave as little room for error as possible, because, as often as not, something goes wrong anyway, despite all your precautions.

Tournament fishing days can sometimes stretch well beyond sunset, to midnight or beyond—as I can personally testify—if, for example, a shaft suddenly breaks, a propeller bends or throws a blade, a rudder drops, or an engine just stops doing its job. It may be Murphy's Law—or just Neptune's way of finding out if you have what it takes to be a man in his kingdom, the roughest, moodiest, and biggest on earth. Either way, something will inevitably go wrong or malfunction during a competition with so many boats.

But just as surely as you felt an acute sense of disappointment, when you limp back to port at midnight, tired and frustrated with a mishap, immediately you feel a heart-swelling sense of gratitude seeing the diver, or the mechanic, waiting at the dock, eager to fix what went wrong. After all, this is not a competition, this is *the competition*, when camaraderie and support are at their best.

Why do they make the sacrifice to come that late at night and stay until the problem is solved? It's simple: they are dedicated professionals and loyal friends, and it's showtime. That's the Open, too, just as much as the race offshore and the inevitable mechanical failure or storm or exhaustion. While they are busy fixing whatever went wrong with *Caribeña*, I can take a break resembling a nap. I will be ready to go again, before the sun gives the skies the first pink-ish hint that it is about to rise. With the malfunctions reme-died and the diver or mechanic already gone, I always find a handwritten note left behind that simply says: "Propeller changed" or "Engine running well now." And, invariably, "Good luck!"

And how much do I owe to the crew at Cropper Oil? Gen-erally, when they go around refueling all the boats, *Caribeña* is still out at sea or, if semi-disabled, hobbling back home, too late for her single tank to be refilled. But once back in port, when I wake from my usual nap at 4:00 A.M. and check the fuel gauge, the needle resting on full tells me the crew has been back in the middle of the night, ensuring me a chance to go out again. There is no doubt that they all are the honorary members of *Caribeña*'s fishing team, and the Open is enriched for me because I compete for them as well as for myself.

It was early in the afternoon when I decided to go back to *Caribeña* to start rigging my baits. A slight breeze ruffled the dark water, and hungry gulls cried overhead as the tourna-ment's console boat returned me to *Caribeña*.

I had brought out three small boxes with twelve new hooks each and started filing their points to a razor sharpness when I felt that I was being observed. I turned around. The two boys on the dock behind me didn't move or say a word, but they took in every detail.

"Hi guys."

Only one weak "Hi" was returned.

"How you doing?"

Nothing this time.

"Are you in the tournament?"

"No."

"Would you like to come aboard? You can help me if you want."

Seldom do I invite people to come on my boat, and usually the last thing I want is help from those at the dock. I have my systems—as when rigging bait or docking and handling the lines—and I implement them in particularly precise sequences that work for me.

But I'm a soft touch with kids, and boy, they were quick to jump aboard—an eight-year-old named Paul and an even younger fellow named Johnny, who both lived nearby. I showed them how to cut mono for leaders and put them to work. "These pieces of thicker line are used to connect the fish hook at one end and the lighter fishing line on the reel at the other end," I told them. I read "why" in their eyes and explained, "The thicker line is rated one hundred pound. I used it for leaders. The fishing line alone, at twenty pounds, wouldn't last the first marlin attack. So, the leader is necessary to withstand the chafing abuse inflicted by a hooked marlin's bill."

I like my leaders five feet long for going after white marlin, and the boys did a fine job cutting equal lengths, severing the line with Hi-Seas fisherman pliers from a gray monofilament coil of 100-pound Jinkai, the supple Japanese fishing line I favor to withstand the marlin's acrobatic dance. The boys made twenty-four of these leaders. Then, for blue marlin, they cut another ten leaders, each twenty feet long, from a 300-pound test roll.

Paul and Johnny took their jobs seriously. And when the work was well done, I let them know that I was grateful. I assigned them the task of aligning hooks and leaders by size. They seated themselves on the teak lid of my empty fish box lying across *Caribeña*'s cockpit and sorted through the hooks, then lined up the monofilament leaders before they were crimped to either end of the line. I would finish the job on the leaders later, out at the fishing grounds, with a loop—a no-name knot tied at the hookless end. I would keep the leaders unlooped to the line until the last minute, in case I decided to add a short colorful skirt to the ballyhoo I typically rigged as bait.

It was a warm afternoon. Islands of silence appeared occasionally in our easy flow of talk about lines, hooks, reels, rods, bait, and the purpose of each.

"Yes," I answered Paul's question about a leader. "It will hold a b-i-i-i-i-g marlin. . . . No! It won't break. . . . Exactly! The drag won't let those two get too far apart. . . . No! It isn't too small. A number-five hook is all I need to catch a white marlin."

The boys were curious about bait. "Just small ballyhoos," I told them. "A few mullets, and some horses will do." *Horses?* "That's what these are called: horse ballyhoos. They can be twice as big as the regular ballyhoo. And blue marlin seem to like them as an appetizer, before they can catch a big mahimahi or tuna for their serious meal."

I picked up a rigged bait. "This is a large horse ballyhoo with a number eight hook, rigged with the three-hundred-pound monofilament leader you just cut. No blue marlin could resist this morsel."

The boys were impressed by size. Johnny hinted that "the hooks used in *other* boats" are much bigger than mine.

"And the mates have rigged big mackerel for bait!" Paul exclaimed.

I shook my head. "No," I insisted, "I like the way horse ballyhoo moves when trolled from the center rigger."

A svelt woman walked toward us down the docks, and Johnny suddenly looked up. "Here comes my mom," he said. I had heard that his parents were divorcing; Johnny, apparently, was the only man in her life.

She greeted us with a simple "Hi!" but the greeting floated like a song. She looked at me, then turned to her son. "Do not disturb Mr. Carlos," she told him. And to me: "Send him away if he bothers you."

"He's not bothering me," I assured both mother and son. And that was the truth. "He's helping me."

She smiled. It was a simple response, but my eyes had carried an inquisitive message that her soft look found and seemed to answer. Shy—but not too shy. She was getting divorced, I reminded myself. I had been there myself. Twice. I knew what she was going through, and, looking at her, I knew I would be there if she wanted to talk. "We will be done in fifteen minutes, and I will be ready to go for a drink around five o'clock," I said, pausing to see how I was doing. "Would you like to come?" I asked her.

"I would love it," she said, "but I can't. My mother is in town for dinner." She hesitated. "But I can come back at eight o'clock," she added uncertainly. "Would that be too late?"

"Not at all. That would be a perfect time."

The boys remained immersed in their work, not surprisingly, oblivious to what had just taken place. After all, at their age, fishing tackle was much more interesting than girls. They were thrilled that they had been granted permission to come aboard, allowed to inspect the basic details of my secrets with bait, and received an answer to every question they dared to ask. But they would have to pay a price: we had things to put away.

"OK, guys. That's it for today. Now it's time to put it all back where it belongs. Sort the hooks by size, same for the egg sinks. (Yes, those egg-shaped pieces of lead that make the bait seem to swim when fastened under its chin.) Coil the line, pick up the copper wire that secures the bait to the hook, and please, pass me the salt." I always finish my rigging by thoroughly sprinkling kosher salt over the silvery bellies of the bait fish. They rested on their backs atop the cotton towel covering the blocks of ice in the bait box. The salt was particularly important, since few marlin had been caught in recent days, and I anticipated that during the tournament, the bait would be trolled, untouched, for long periods. The salt would help to keep the ballyhoo swimming through *Caribeña*'s wake without being washed out and coming apart—so that they would appear, in a way, full of life.

"Watch that knife!" I warned Johnny. "Don't make it happy! It enjoys itself when it cuts!"

It took some time to put things away and get organized again, even with the benefit of four extra hands. The boys had become part of my dock team. Theirs would be the first two pairs of eyes to spot my boat coming back, looking to see if I was flying any of the flags that indicated a catch. Theirs would be the first voices I would hear when I approached the crowded dock.

I thanked them for their help and assured them that, as always, I would do my best with the bait we had just rigged. It was Sunday, August 4th. Twenty minutes shy of 5:00 P.M. Time to get ready. A shower wouldn't eliminate all the smell the bait had left on my hands; for that, I needed to use my special orange compound of liquid soap with particles of sand. It masks, although it can never entirely eradicate, the fishy aroma that is simply part of my skin during this week.

Next, I went back to the tournament hub to complete the registration process. Unlike earlier in the day, there were only ten to twelve people in front of me: two or three friends, and the rest, faces I had seen before. I was last on the registration line. I entered *Caribeña*'s name and then myself—angler, captain, and mate, under a single name.

Jim Motsko, the founder of the tournament, handed me a registration package and a bag containing tags for any fish I might be lucky enough to hook up and reel in. We were, officially, Boat 237—the last entrant of the twenty-third.

"I have a long way to go to be number one," I said to him.

"I don't think so," he laughed. We wished each other luck, then I walked to the captains' meeting, just getting under way. Chuck Motsko, Jim's cousin and codirector of the event, went through the rules. He ended the meeting with an announcement: "It's official. Two hundred and thirty-seven boats will fish the twenty-third White Marlin Open. Close to thirteen hundred anglers will compete in it. Good luck."

As always, I would be the only one fishing alone.

After the captains' meeting, two light drinks, a three hundred-yard stroll, and a combined four hundred smiles, pats on the back and hugs later, it was time to say good night to the guys and their wives and significant others.

Having fifteen minutes to spare before meeting my date, I jumped aboard *Caribeña* to check that everything was fine on board. I verified that she had a full tank of fuel. Batteries had a full charge. I lifted the long cooler top, peeking at the row of rigged baits. They looked great. And so did the rods, ready to bend, and the reels, ready to scream. The boat was in great mechanical shape. I even took time to make a last bimini knot on a reel with new line. I was applying what I had learned fifty years before: to take special care of each and every detail.

I felt prepared.

THREE

·

·

EL DENTUDO

It was my mother who introduced me to fishing a half century ago. She had learned about nature and fishing growing up on a small island, where her own father had been in charge of a towering lighthouse at the mouth of el Rio Uruguay. Her teaching was passionate and warm. I can still see her dexterous, delicate hands, tying all kinds of knots, patiently watching every time I tried. I can still hear her reassuring voice carefully explaining what she had learned so well fishing for *boga* and *pati* from the shores of Martin Garcia island.

Tying those first knots is one of my earliest memories. It was 1945, and my mother, already a veteran angler, was not quite thirty yet, and a mother of two boys. I was almost four, her younger son, a fisherman in the making, entranced by bamboo poles, colorful floats, thin lines, and the simple knots she taught me in preparation for the big day when I would finally get to dip a line.

The scene was a family picnic. At the time, I didn't know about the war raging around the world. Nor could I have known much about the adverse economic impact being felt by my neutral country, Uruguay, or the rippling effects reaching my family, then in the middle of a large middle class. It wouldn't be the right choice of words to say we were poor, but I suspect we didn't have much if you only counted material possessions.

Although public school was free for all and good enough for most, my brother and I, six years apart, attended private schools, receiving a traditional education from the Brothers of El Sagrado Corazón and the Basque priests of Los Vascos de la Immaculada Concepción. They taught us Latin and more French, and we played some soccer (the students out-playing the teachers) and handball (here, they had their revenge). These under-the-cassock-pants-wearing gentle-tough guys were famous disciplinarians in Uruguay. Practitioners of introspection, these religious men would look for balance, mixing academics with the outdoors, and though fishing was not one of their pastimes, that search for equilibrium—taught by example and learned by osmosis—may have something to do with the person I am today: an active observer of life at land, a roaming monk of the deep sea.

———

Unlike public school and dreams, milk, bread, and ice came at a price during those years. Long rectangular blocks of ice were delivered door-to-door to keep aliments fresh in the cooling box that was to the refrigerator what smoke signals became to the telegraph, and typewriters to word processors. Food was bought daily from the string of vendors roaming the streets of our neighborhood *en la ciudad de* Montevideo, the capital of Uruguay.

Founded in 1726 on the northern shores of El Rio de la Plata, this small and charming town had preserved much of its quaint Spanish colonial appearance, particularly en la Ciudad Vieja—the old town district by the city port—its houses with thick walls, corniced façades, and Morisco's balconies with elaborated ironwork, aging across one another over centuries of history and mute narrow streets. The city retained the styles and customs of the past. Among these were delivery carts pulled by a single horse over uneven *calles adoquinadas*—the cobblestone streets in my own neighborhood. There were also four-wheeled beer wagons, always pulled by teams of four to six gigantic Clydesdales *de color cerveza*, descendants of the famous breed originated in Scotland. Those *equinos*, like the vast majority of the human population, had at some point immigrated from Western Europe to this subtropical land known for centuries as *La Banda Oriental del Uruguay*, or the East Bank of the Uruguay River, a 300- by 350-mile territory, a gem of undulating green pastures festooned to the south and east by a string of golden sandy beaches, set between the South America giants of Argentina and Brazil.

Of course, there were also automobiles all over Montevideo, mostly Fords and Chevrolets, but they were few in our *barrio*, and, for certain, none belonged to my family at that time.

For this family picnic, we traveled by streetcar to the national park known as *La Barra del Río Santa Lucía*. Armed with a traditional picnic load and two protruding bamboo fishing rods, we sped out of the city, the streetcar drinking energy from the electric cable above its roof.

Passengers' bodies wobbled, involuntarily dancing to the swaying rhythm of the train. It was hot inside the crowded car, and I was glad to have a window seat; the air seeping through the open window cooled my face and chest and helped to dissipate the heat rising through the floor under my shoeless feet. Outside the city limits, the houses dwindled to a few; inside, the travelers' laughter intensified. Before I knew it, the train pulled to a stop. We had arrived.

Many relatives had gathered for the day outdoors. Everyone was happy: talking, gesturing, smiling, and laughing, whether sitting or standing around wooden tables filled with some enticing samples of homemade appetizers, and a colorful collection of *botellas de refrescos*, wine, beer, and soda, helping us to get cool and celebrate.

The party could easily have bored me; after all, I wasn't old enough to drink—in Uruguay the normal age to have wine at home with your folks must have been six or so. And I was not mature enough to understand *los cuentos verdes*, the off-color jokes provoking rolls of laughter from the older crowd. Nor was I strong enough to swim in the river as did many of the older children. But my mother's wisdom in bringing those fishing poles did more for me than save the day. Standing together with her at the edge of *el Río Santa Lucía*, she and I fished together for the very first time.

I wonder now if she had been nervous, if she had even prayed, not for the sake of catching fish to roast over the coals but to avoid the unthinkable fiasco of not catching a fish.

I watched everything she did. Like her, I repeatedly whipped the water with the upper part of the rod, producing a noisy, splashing commotion. "Noise in the water attracts curious fish," she said, repeating the splashing. "We have to tell the fish that lunch is served. Come and have a bite."

The lady spoke the truth. As she was telling me to concentrate on my float, hers started to wobble and dance.

"*Está picando!* (It's biting!)" she announced in a quiet voice while her float accelerated its tilted walk before being dragged underwater. She bent forward over the spot, put some slack in her line, and suddenly and rapidly lifted her hand and forearm, jerking the rod with a quick, short motion, producing the hook up that makes the line come taut. What ensued was pure magic: I saw the yarn cutting the water with a swift run as the thin tip of the homemade rod bent

69

into an arch. When my mother pulled the rod up, this time with a triumphant laugh, there it was—a fish!

"Un bagre," she announced. It had seemed to come out of nowhere, wiggling, suspended in mid-air, for me, a revelation, the perfect definition of what fishing was. As soon as my mother landed it on the riverbank, before we could say anything else, it was *my* turn to act. *My* float did the tip-tip-tip dance, preceding the short tilted walk, and then, dipping down, disappeared just as hers had done. I felt the persistent and glorious *tip-tip, tip-tip-tip* telegraphed through my bamboo cane as it bowed to the jerks. And imitating all my mother's actions of seconds before, I, too, produced the magic trick: a wild wiggling *bagre amarillo!* as long as my extended arm and as thick as my own leg.

That was a big fish—for a guy my size. While I didn't have my mother's skill, nor her grace in touch or stance, I did have big lungs to send around my jubilation as the wiggler danced in front of my eyes—ten inches of pure gold catfish.

For a whole hour—that seemed only ten minutes or so—my mother and I kept landing those yellow catfish, one bigger than the next. "We need twelve for lunch," she said. We caught fifteen. The tricky part wasn't catching but unhooking them without being lacerated by the rigid point of the first ray of their dorsal and pectoral fins. My mother, being a mother, didn't let me try to remove the barbless hooks.

My cousin Armín—a grown man with children my age—

and Mirta, his wife, cleaned and filleted the fish, immediately submerging them in a concoction of beer, orange juice, and lemon juice that my mother had prepared well in advance, confident of our catch.

As I remember, everything went well until it was time to break for lunch. I didn't want to quit. Who, among serious fishermen, would dare to quit in the height of the bite? And for lunch?

"We have to go, sit down and have lunch with the rest of the family, but we'll come back for *mojarras*," my mother said to convince me to stop fishing, which I reluctantly did.

My father was in charge of the large, inclined grill. Under his watchful eye, the meats of a typical *parrillada* were laid away from the intense heat. They were the butchered insides of the beef, like *riñones, chinchulines y mollejas*, their names better left *en español* to concentrate on their taste. Next to them were our famous *chorizos*—the traditional sausages made with white pork and red meats finely chopped and properly seasoned. Frequently basted with *chimichurri*—the renowned aromatic vinaigrette sauce for grilled meats. All of them, including the black *morcillas* (blood sausages), dripped their juices over the coals, the resulting puffs of smoke permeating the park's air.

My father enjoyed his job. Comfortable and relaxed, in shorts, sporting a large red-and-blue bandanna around his neck, he had spent much of the morning with a fork in his right hand while keeping in his left a glass of robust homemade wine. Putting it aside (but not too far), he served the clan.

For the fish my mother and I caught, he reserved a separate grill. I had a first sense of primitive pride in having made a contribution to the family and myself.

After lunch, my mother and I went back to the river shore, this time changing the bait from worms to heart meat, and catching some three- and four-inch *mojarras*, though considerably smaller than the catfish, still made a great catch. Small as they were, we needed a hundred of them. Properly kept on ice borrowed from the containers that had housed the sodas and beer, these *mojarras* would serve us well fried up at home the following day.

Wrapped in her proud maternal hug, borderline four, I felt like a man.

●

●

●

That first fishing trip was followed by an outing to the East Coast and the Atlantic Ocean later that summer. My father took us to the station, then my mother, my brother, and I boarded the train in Montevideo. Tía Clarita, my mother's aunt, and Clarita's daughter, Blanquita, met us at the train station in the rustic city of Maldonado, fewer than 100 miles away.

Even before *la locomotora* exhaled to a complete stop, my mother recognized our relatives and called to them in an excited voice. "There they are! There they are!"

We squeezed toward the nearest door. I, the first to disembark, jumped onto the concrete platform, landing in a sea of hugs, kisses, and laughter, embraced by the two euphoric women and licked by the little black dog that Blanquita held in her arms. The effusive initial greetings were quickly followed by inquiries about each other's husbands. Tía Clarita's "was too busy with his daily routine. He would meet us at the house." My mother's, Salvador, an insurance inspector with American Century in Uruguay, "had an ill-timed deadline, impossible to postpone." Such were the excuses the women exchanged to justify absent men.

"But don't worry!" my mother said laughing. "He intends to join us toward the end of the week."

Outside the station, we boarded a taxicab. It didn't take long to cruise through the city of Maldonado, "a pearl by the water in a string of sixteenth-century Spanish colonial settlements that remains virtually unchanged by the passage of time," wrote my mother in a postcard I found years later. At the center of downtown was the Catholic Church towering over the square, a small public garden sprinkled with white benches and filled with pigeons, which constantly flew between the square, the church, and the train station a few blocks away.

I quickly grew to like Tía Clarita and the rest of her family, the playful puppy dog, her large hospitable home, and the food. Every morning we would have breakfast seated on benches alongside a sturdy, rectangular table supported by square, green legs. My mother's uncle had made it from local oak with the impressive carpenter's tools he kept in the barn. One rainy day, I saw him working with the handsaw and the jack plane, making a wooden doghouse. He was determined to have the growing little dog live outside. "Here is where he should sleep, not in the kitchen," he said, driving the nails into the wood.

The kitchen was huge, the ceiling low, the floor made of slate. It was my preferred part of the house. The plastered walls were white, the beams dark, and both rough, in contrast with the ambiance: soft and smooth. There was time to talk and laugh.

The well-kept garden was full of amazing smells: the aroma of pale blue clusters of wisteria flowers cascading from the frame of the house and yellowish honeysuckle swarming over the fence. I felt like a hummingbird, regretting that the flowers didn't taste as good as they smelled. However pleasant the aroma of the flowers, it was the orchard that became the main attraction. I enjoyed the sweetness found in the ripened abundant fruits—another country novelty for this visiting city boy. The guava was my favorite. I combed the foliage everyday, hands searching for round, soft, green, deliciously mellow fruits.

But all this paled next to the excitement I felt while fishing at La Barra, a short car ride from Maldonado. The river, the adjacent lagoons, and the wonderful beaches around Punta del Este were our destinations. The sands and waters of these Atlantic beaches called *Playa Mansa* and *Playa*

Brava were finer and clearer than those of Montevideo and the familiar Santa Lucia to the west.

Grasping my bamboo rod with both hands, the water above my knees, the incoming waves wetting my chest, I cast bait into the calm water of *Playa Mansa*, as close as I could to a cut by the sandbar where the waves started to swell, yards away from their final break behind my back. My mother said that small and large *anchoa* or bluefish, *roncaderas* and *pejerrey*, and the occasional *pámpano* come in with the incoming tide, and so did sand sharks and larger black drums, all finding their way through those cuts close to shore.

"Where is the cut?" I asked.

"Just there," she said, pointing out to an invisible spot some twenty yards away. "See where the waves start to grow? See the space between them, there, in the middle, where it's flat? That's where the cuts are. And the reason the water doesn't rise like the rest of the wave is because the submerged sandbar is broken there, allowing the water to come in unobstructed. That cut is like an open door for the fish. Once they cross it and are inside, between the sandbar and the proper shore, the fish tend to travel in that canal, following the tide. They come to eat the smaller fish. You will improve your chances of catching a fish by casting close to the cut, for the first food they'll see might be your bait."

Observing her own float, my mother often checked the one on my line, smiling when her eyes encountered mine, her silent way of sharing patience and hope for the task at hand. Reassured, I would wait for that hallowed instant when the fish finally dignified the bait with a bite.

Those waters of the Maldonado coasts are greatly influenced by the currents and winds of the Atlantic. The higher salinity meant different species of fish: *pejerrey, roncaderas,* and *burel*—juvenile bluefish—replaced the familiar *bagres amarillos y mojarras* found to the west. I quickly learned that these fish prefer different bait—shrimp, crab, and strips of squid—which we served at different depths by properly adjusting the distance between hook and float. Each variety had its own peculiar bite—though subtle similarities could confuse a novice angler. With my mother's advice, I learned over time to distinguish small details, mastering the kind of bait preferred by each species, the telltale bites, and the techniques that would produce frequent and consistent hook ups.

In an age when it seemed that time barely moved, I perceived that week in Maldonado going too fast. I remember being happy with my father's arrival but distraught when the weekend for departure was upon us. And, despite the speedy train, the return trip to Montevideo seemed slow.

The summer was over, and during the fall and loathsome winter, which in the Southern Hemisphere runs from March until the end of August, my relief from the routine of school was the promise that, by early September, we would all be able to feel and see the first signs of spring.

The winter days in that region of the southern cone, under the influence of the Antarctic winds, were short, often
rainy, and mostly dark. In the days before television and
with only one radio in the house, I ended most days listen-
ing to my mother as she read from a book or recounted an interesting tale. My favorite was the one about *El Dentudo*.

"Once upon a time, there was a BIG FISH roaming the
deep lagoon formed at the bend of the rumbling creek," my
mother said. "He was BIG . . ."

"How big?" I always interrupted.

"This big . . ." She stretched her arms as far apart as she
could.

"*Muy grande,*" I said, nodding.

Retracting her arms and resting her left hand over my
arm, with the other still raised, she added, "And not only
that big, but with TEETH THIS LARGE," putting a vertical inch of space between the fingertips of her curved index
finger and thumb, forming the letter "C" as in cruel, crip-
pling, crunch.

Following her gesturing hands, my wide eyes would
move from head to tail at least twice before converging on
that invisible tooth that she held in mid-air in front of my
face. I imagined rows of them, side by side, bony hard,
white, and pointy, ready to bite. With my overactive boy's
imagination, I envisioned the monstrous proportions of the
silvery-dark, fast-swimming nightmare.

"He was an angry predator," my mother continued, "in

relentless and hunger-driven pursuit of any fish that swam within his reach in the lagoon. One single bite was enough to cut his chosen meal in two."

She was a master of the dramatic pause, which gave my imagination free reign to complete the image of the big, bad fish, full of rage, chasing around the poor bait or, if it chose, any larger fish that dared to swim close.

"No wonder all the other fishes were afraid of *El Dentudo de la Laguna* 'Big Tooth of the Lagoon,'" she said, "the fearless monster that was merciless at best." As she rolled the list of its numerous prey off her tongue and explained details of their habits, I felt something I couldn't describe at that time; later, I realized I hankered for "The Challenge" to go out and kick the scales off the beast.

"He is still in the lagoon, well fed and bigger than ever." My mother described the gigantic head of silvery steel, with a cold, brilliant black eye on each side—the size of *un real de plata* (a silver quarter) set above the powerful, elongated jaws and the sinister mouth that, without ever emitting a single sound, was always ready to deliver the kiss of death. The head, like every other fish, lacking a neck, is directly attached to the torpedo-shaped body, without a waistline, ending in a wide-scalloped tail, the powerful engine that propelled a sleek killing machine.

"*Paaahh!*" I responded, the Spanish equivalent of "Wow!"

"With the unusual winter drought, there is no way for the prey to escape. The lagoon is no longer connected to the creek, the small tributary of the much wider winding river which connects to the sea."

"Is there a larger fish that might eat the beast?" I asked with faint hope.

"Not a chance. He's the biggest and the meanest of them all. And the rain has flooded the big river of the north, which has brought the big fish to the lagoon. For sure one big fish was brought with that flood. But, according to some other reports, two may have been washed down by the flood, for two gigantic concentric ripples were seen on the surface at the same time, thirty feet apart."

"Were there two? Or only one? Do you know for sure?"

"Nobody knows . . . yet," she said. "Some believe the one swims so fast it could have made both ripples while chasing two different bait fish, almost at the same time."

I was speechless.

"But one or two, the fact remains: we are losing all our small fish, and some of the larger ones too . . ." She added resolutely, "too many, perhaps . . ."

Departing from the narrative of that repeated story one night, she asked, "Would you like to do something about that?"

"Yes! . . . but how?"

"Well, we can go fishing again, if you like, only this time, not to catch small fish as we have done in the past, but to catch *El Dentudo* himself. We can arm ourselves with a good, strong, two-piece rod, which I have already seen at the store.

A long fishing line if it's thick enough will give us a real chance to lift him, and we will make a very nice float out of that champagne cork that I kept from last Christmas."

"I know where it is," I said, proudly. "It's in the drawer of the sewing machine."

"You're right!" She smiled at my interruption. "My father taught me how to make a hole through the cork with a red-hot nail. We will do that very carefully, and we will pass the hollow quill of an old ostrich feather through it, the whole thing to be threaded by the twisted fishing line. It will help us to adjust the depth at which we will be fishing the bait, and we will paint our new float red and white, to make it visible even in the twilight. For this guy, we are going to have a real hook—one of those with a long shank, with a barb, and an off bite—if we are to get a firm hold on his jaw once he dares to attack our bait."

"Wow!"

"Now we have something to prove. We will try to catch him for the sake of the other fish but also for ourselves. Next month, just before the arrival of spring, we will celebrate your father's birthday. Remember? September nineteenth. If we can catch *El Dentudo*, we will cook him for your father.

"Once caught," she continued, "we will squeeze, all over the fish, orange and lemon juice before baking it in the oven, with butter, white pepper, garlic, slices of lemon, fresh parsley, and white wine. The fish will be served over a bed of white rice prepared with salted butter, adding lentils, diced red peppers, pitless green olives, capers, and chunks of walnuts, with a side of hot stuffed potatoes. And we will feel very good, for we will have saved all the other fish—a ton of them—from the awful fate of becoming lunch for a creature who doesn't even belong in the same lagoon."

On my first fishing trip, I had become acquainted with the single-piece, still-green bamboo pole, with flexible tip. We had attached to it, with a double square knot, a long, homey piece of sewing thread going through an adjustable pierced cork that, in more glamorous times, had known the smooth kiss of a young merlot. Almost two feet down from the cork with the fading red-tinted mark, exactly at the very end of the "fishing line," dangled a formerly straight pin that had been bent into a barbless hook.

That had been all the tackle I had needed up to that point to catch *mojarras* and catfish. But that wintry night in August, some fifty years ago, my mother must have thought I was ready to be pushed into a higher league, be armed with better tools, go out, hunt the "big fish," and, in the process, become a big boy. I was fascinated by the prospects of getting a new rod and hook. She penciled drawings of the new tools.

"Three weeks from today it will be one week before *la luna nueva*, the new moon," she said. "And with half the moon reflecting the sun's light, we should fish the crepuscular hours. Three weeks to the *cuarto menguante*, the last quarter moon will be sooner than you might think." Then she turned off the light beside my bed as I rolled over on my side. I vaguely heard her say "good night." As I slid into a deep sleep, with a wonderful brand-new rod in my hand, I dreamed that night of setting the hook in the bony mouth of Big Tooth.

·

·

·

Years later, I would find other sites to cast in search of excitement. At Punta Carretas, I would fish from a group of dark-greenish rocks piercing the estuary. I would tempt *corvinas* arriving in a rising tide to take a clean bite of my fresh bait, three- to four-inch-long raw shrimp inserted to camouflage the shank and throat of the hook, leaving only the sharp metal point exposed. For the fish, this looked like an easy meal—better than digging with their rubbery thick lips for oblong white clams half buried in the surrounding sands, and much better than scraping black mussel shells off razor-sharp rocks. Sometimes, I ended up the fool, wasting the shrimp that my mother could have used in the kitchen. Other times, I was able to trade the small shrimp for a big fish, and oh, the excitement when the shrimp lured a fish to bite! The distinctive pull of a *corvina* grinding the shrimp with its powerful molars far down in its throat never failed to send a strong message through the fishing line, the unequivocally clear "I am here to eat." My immediate and assertive response, "I am here to catch," was almost always followed by a battle of wills: the fish determined to escape; I determined to reel her in.

Half the challenge was not to lose the fish on the protruding, cultrated rocks that, sharp as knives, loved to cut mono-filament lines. On a good day, a few *corvinas*, roughly fifteen to twenty pounds each, would end up in my mother's kitchen. But there were numerous days when the high tides didn't co-incide with my fishing times, or days when the *corvina* or the *anchoa* would boycott my baited hook as if they sensed that the camouflaged "shrimp dance" in the undercurrent of the flood tide would be fatal for them. Those days, the telegraph-ing line, like the reel itself, would turn utterly silent.

Even on those days, I would still enjoy the quiet solitude. When the bait failed to get a fishy kiss from my prey, I might have been momentarily disappointed, but I never returned home dejected, for catching might have been the goal—but it was not the game. I thought the worst I could do playing this outdoor game was "tie," for in fishing, there is no such thing as defeat. My mind would wander, mesmerized by the rhythm of waves and tides.

On these trips, it did occur to me that my actions were bringing death to other living things. Death had flown close to home: My godmother, a slender woman with a big warm smile, long fingers that stroked my head, and waist-long ebony hair, had, without warning, become sick and died. Her passing left unbearable sorrow for everyone who knew her. *"Es el destino,"* my mother told me. "Everybody has his own fate. You have to accept that."

Standing on the hard rocks of Punta Carretas, I learned to accept that death is the natural sequence to life.

While many of my peers were playing together, I had begun at this early age to realize the pleasures of being alone. At school, and around home, my friends would have long-distance races. However much I enjoyed the competition, I soon learned that I preferred running even more when I was alone, cutting through the open fields, feeling invigorated by the resistance of the air and, yet, racing to nowhere in particular, for when I raced alone, there was no finish line. I could spend hours alone practicing with a soccer ball, learning to put just the right spin on it, so that toward the end of its flight, it would curve in, or out, or drop suddenly like a baseball does after leaving the hands of a great breaking-ball pitcher.

My imagination and introspection were also enhanced by the reading I did as a youngster. I read everything within reach, including *La Tribuna Popular*, the morning conservative paper, and *El Diario*, the evening liberal paper. Occasionally, I would have access to *Reader's Digest, en español,* one of my favorites. From its pages, I learned about Oscar Wilde, Bernard Shaw, and Mark Twain. I also read about *The Old Man and the Sea* before that Sunday when I went to the matinee to see Spencer Tracy in the role of Santiago catching the gigantic blue marlin. Being twelve or so, I thought, "A fish that huge can't exist!"

Neruda's poems were around the house. And so was Rodó's prose. My mother sighed with the poetry found in the *Rimas de Becquer*, while José Hernández's *Martin Fierro* became my father's favorite book, so much so that he learned by heart many of its six-line stanzas. In a way, they were the Frosts, Hemingways, and Updikes of my country. All these books and magazines had my priority, unlike assigned schoolbooks. There was, however, one exception: Giuffra's geography, my early window to the vast world: how my thumbs carefully let go edge after edge of each page, my eyes consuming figures, pictures, and maps.

Fishing, thinking, running, reading, reflecting, and dreaming: these early experiences deeply influenced my later life. Being with family and friends has, for the most part, been delightful and rewarding. Family and friends have been important. But, at the same time, I have found it equally important to find my inner self: to take care of myself.

My father, a product of his time, a sort of bon vivant and gallivant—otherwise a very decent man—tried to teach me only the good things he was himself so good at: "Be honest, be open, be respectful, be loving, show consideration, and call things by their names." I've tried to live up to those rules. And my mother—the loving soul, the moral model, the guardian of manners and etiquette—by instilling her love of fishing in me also taught me to listen to my own inner voice, to seek solitude, and to cherish what I found in my search. I learned the pleasures of an overnight bonfire on a solitary beach while I fished at night for *pejerrey*, with a hand-held net of fine mesh and a kerosene lamp on the other hand to lure the curious fish with the dim light—the warm summer water up to my chest.

Those who touched, shaped, or guided my early years are gone now, but not from my memory, not from my life. I still "talk" to them—particularly during those contemplative moods induced by my ocean trips. Where else is life so insistently reduced to its primary elements? Where else can I sense so intensely the basic nature of my own needs?

This aspect of fishing is both a physical and a spiritual need. I need it like I need the air I breathe. In solitude, I find my way and gain strength. I get in touch with myself. I build my inner church. And back on shore, I share what I have learned.

FOUR

·

·

BEYOND
DIAMOND SHOALS

The day I first discovered marlin fishing, I was not roaming offshore in *Caribeña* but, rather, comfortably settled in my favorite armchair in my home in Virginia, next to a roaring fire that danced wild and bright in the fireplace. I had just completed an assignment for Voice of America, and I was enjoying a break. I turned the pages of a fishing magazine, and there it was. A marlin so gigantic, so impressive, it instantly reminded me of the one I saw in a Spencer Tracy movie years before. I could hardly believe the size of that fish in the picture next to the guy holding the rod, wearing a huge smile of triumph.

It was December 1970, and everything I knew about fishing was about to change. "June is the month to catch one like this: a blue marlin of 600 pounds" read the caption next to the photo. For me, then almost thirty years younger than I am now and as many pounds lighter, the marlin was more than a fish. It was a dream to be chased.

"Blue marlin," I wrote inside the cover of a book of matches, followed by the name of the captain from the ad and his telephone number, unaware I was about to meet destiny on a blind date.

I made the long-distance phone call. And as we talked— I with my south-of-the-border Spanglish, he with his Carolina drawl—our accents clashed, but we agreed that on a certain day in the middle of June, he would take me offshore in his charter boat to fish for blue marlin.

Fate had dealt its hand, and I found myself making plans to go to North Carolina. The captain would be waiting for me on his boat in Hatteras, a small town on the Outer Banks of that southern coastal state, 250 miles south-southeast of McLean, where I was living.

Whiling away the cold, short days of January and February, and the blustery winds of March, I read details about the art of pursuing billfish. I learned the blue marlin's scientific name, *Makaira nigricans,* its migratory habits, its favorite foods, and its preferred water temperature range, above seventy-five degrees.

I became very interested in the different species of billfish. The blue marlin, I found, is the largest in the Atlantic with its stocky body, long bill, trailing dorsal fin, retractable pectoral fins, and two keels (rather than one, like the swordfish). This marlin rarely gathers in schools, feeds mainly on fishes, likes small tuna and mahimahi, preys on octopus and squid, and apparently cannot resist a well-rigged horse ballyhoo.

The Atlantic blue marlin is one of nine species of billfish. Of the other eight, four are found in the Atlantic: the white marlin, the sailfish, the spearfish, and the swordfish. The black marlin and the striped marlin are species found only in the Pacific. The other two billfish recognized as a separate species are the Pacific blue marlin and the Pacific sailfish. The swordfish is a unique species, and its distribution is worldwide. There might be some subtypes of each of these species.

The easiest way to tell a blue marlin from a white is to look at the shape of its dorsal fin tip. In the blue, the tip is pointed sharply, and the fin usually lacks rounded black spots.

In the case of a white marlin, the dorsal is broadly rounded, while its brother (or cousin) known as the hatchet marlin (considered a white marlin) is squared off, not pointed or rounded. The white marlin may have many black spots on the membrane of this fin; it also has a single lateral line, arched below the high part of the dorsal fin, extending straight tailward. While the world-record white is a 181-pound fish caught off the coast of Vitoria, in Brazil, the majority of these marlin are in the 45-pound range and can be found only in the Atlantic, from Maine to southern Brazil.

The spearfish, with its short bill, is perhaps the smallest

of the billfish, weighing some twenty-five pounds. It's rarely caught in the mid-Atlantic. Its low dorsal fin is just the opposite of the sailfish's dorsal, the sail's great fin being the largest and most spectacular among the billfish of the world. The average weight of the Atlantic sail is thirty-five to forty pounds, while the Pacific sailfish being caught nowadays is usually eighty pounds or more.

The spearfish roams the Mediterranean, venturing to the western Atlantic. Two or three may be caught every other year off the coast of Ocean City. White and blue marlin, sailfish, and spearfish, as well as the mighty swordfish, can be found between 40 fathoms and 1,000 fathoms. There's still some disagreement among some biologists as to whether there are one, two, or four kinds of blue marlin in the world's oceans. South and North Atlantic populations and Atlantic and Pacific stocks have been thought of as separate species in the past, but today the consensus seems to be that the Atlantic and Pacific populations are one species. In any case, our blue wanders from Maine through the Gulf and Caribbean, and the South Atlantic populations straggle down to Uruguay. The greatest concentrations seem to be around the Virgin Islands, the Caribbean, in the Gulf of Mexico, especially off the mouth of the Mississippi River, and in the Brazil current off South America.

The king of Atlantic marlins, the blue, is often over ten feet in length. Males rarely exceed 300 pounds, but females grow much larger, often doubling and tripling the weight of the males. Maryland's record blue weighed 942 pounds, caught in 1989 by Dr. Jim Daniels aboard my friend Captain Marty Moran's Bertram, *Memory Maker*. In North Carolina, four or five blues have been caught that weighed more than 1,000 pounds. The first ever was caught on Harry Baum's *Jo Boy;* another was caught by Slim Flinchum, a late member of the Ocean City Light Tackle Club, on his *Allison*.

Like other billfish, blue marlin are migratory, closely tied to warm waters. They follow their source of food across the seasons and the movements of the major ocean currents, which, in the Northern Hemisphere, spin poleward from the tropics. Though they may be found on the high seas thousands of miles from the continents, they also approach within a few miles of coastal regions with adjacent deep water, like Hawaii.

As with so many of our giant oceanic species, blue marlin have come under intense pressure from long-liners, especially the Japanese and Cubans, who together harvest about 1,000 tons of marlin annually from the Caribbean region. Within 200 miles of the U.S. coasts, their vessels are required to release all billfish captured, but the marlin they catch are dead or too damaged to recover.

During the summer months, Hatteras is an ideal place for the blue marlin; the warm waters of the Gulf Stream run offshore as close as thirty to thirty-five miles from the Outer Banks; the depth is right, and baitfish are present in abundance. For years, there have been no better seaworthy sportfishing boats than those built with the famous Carolina flair, and their skippers are, and probably always will be, among the best in the world.

The longer, rainy days of April and those of a flowered, fragrant May were passing slowly, and June was a long time coming. It helped that I was busy at that time with family and work. I was married to a woman who, fortunately, didn't mind my seeking that kind of adventure, and I was also a father to a four-year-old daughter.

Finally, I received a confirmation call from Hatteras. Yes, they were waiting for me, and yes, a few blue marlin already had been caught on other boats.

"Good," I said. "I'm on my way."

Hours later, in the early afternoon, my family and I stopped at Duck, Kitty Hawk, and then Oregon Inlet. The beaches of North Carolina and Uruguay look quite similar; both places are equidistant from the equator—thirty-five degrees north and south—and I felt that the breeze floating over the grassy dunes had been blown north from my native land. In both places pine trees seemed to thrive, lending their distinctive smell to the salty air.

Although we fishermen of Uruguay don't have the famous run of the striped bass to be fished from the surf, we do have black drum *(corvina negra)* that run early in spring and fall, bluefish *(anchoa)*, croaker *(roncadera)*, and red drum *(corvina blanca)*, without the spot on the tail but comparable in size. These are coastal fishes, while tuna *(atún)* and king mackerel *(cavalla)* swim well offshore, beyond the normal range of the few sportfishing boats. The billfish story in that southern latitude still has to be written, for, as far as I know, no one has ever caught a marlin off of Uruguay's Atlantic coast. If the regional billfish species happen to roam south of Brazil—and they might—I suspect they would be out in the deep, some 200 miles offshore, certainly out of range for a day trip on most boats.

On the other hand, in the Northern Hemisphere, off Hatteras, the three most abundant species of billfish swim up and down the migratory highway of the Gulf Stream. Usually they are found there from late May to early October when the sea surface temperatures are above seventy degrees. Blue marlin prefer waters of seventy-six to eighty-one degrees, at least off the mid-Atlantic coast, and it's my personal conviction through repeated experiences that blue marlin are more inclined to bite during the full moons of August and September.

On my first trip to the area, I didn't know what to expect. We took note of Hatteras's houses on the sand dunes built high over wooden pilings—with carports in lieu of first floors—revealing respect for the moods of the ocean at the front door. Experience had taught builders and residents to consider the levels that some raging tides may reach during a storm.

The town of Hatteras is whimsical and charming. The day we arrived, though the rustic marina and the old general store were anchored to the sandy soil, both appeared to be floating in a light mist of salty air. We were tempted to go for a stroll, but it was late and we were tired. The fishing fleet was asleep. So were the evening winds.

The next morning, at the early fishermen's time, after a short car ride and a shorter walk with my daughter and wife, I had no problem finding the marina, abuzz with its restaurant-bar and fishing-tackle-beer-clothing store serving an inviting aromatic breakfast to an eclectic clientele. I approached an old man wearing a once-white cap that was now as gray as the hair that protruded from beneath it. He held a large mug of coffee, and he seemed to be guarding the buffet table. His eyes fixed on my leather sandals, which clearly marked me as a *turista* in his town.

As I came closer to him, I said "Hi," and asked with my eyes a Latin version of the universal "Anybody home?"

"Hello," he said, lifting his cup.

I asked him if he knew the whereabouts of my chartered boat but couldn't understand a word of his response. Finally, extending his arm, with a gnarled, roughened hand that showed the fisherman in him, he pointed out toward the boats on the right side of the marina.

Tired by the lengthy trip, my wife and daughter had declined to have breakfast and had gone back to the car. I ordered a cup of coffee to go and walked toward the cluster of boats. Every one of them was buzzing with activity. Some were just firing up their engines, the exhaust spitting hot water and smoke; a few were already leaving the dock with mates on the bows hanging mooring lines over the piles; and several were majestically sliding away through the mist of the dawn like gigantic white swans. It looked like a live postcard, the vivid colors evoking the most beautiful watercolors of Winslow Homer.

I saw the boat I was to board and greeted the two men aboard. I couldn't have known what they were expecting of me, but I had the feeling they liked it when they learned that I would be the only one coming on board. My family, as interested in offshore fishing as I was interested in sunbathing, remained on the dock, making plans for their free time until my expected return around 5:00 P.M.

I learned from the captain that we were to go some forty miles offshore. I shared this with my family who, ready to leave, shared with me their tentative plans: back to sleep and then a late breakfast, a walk on the beach, a relaxing time under the sun, lunch when and if hungry, and surely a nap before coming back to the dock to see what I might have caught. We hugged and said repeated good-byes. I went back on board, and at the push of a button, the boat's single diesel engine roared to life, as if the eight cylinders were unanimously supporting the spirit of my fighting mood. We left the dock shortly after dawn. The vessel started to plane, and the cockpit trembled under the engine's torque.

Not usually short for words, I still have a hard time expressing the new feelings I was absorbing on my way to the fishing grounds. Ever since that day, I've felt a certain mystique in being around fishing boats, and certainly I was hearing the ocean's irresistible call, an echo of the song I heard as a boy, provoking this adult urge to respond.

Do singing mermaids living offshore call my name? I honestly don't know, but even today I keep hearing that silent call. Maybe there is somewhere embedded in my DNA a lure and seduction to roam the deep seas.

Beyond Diamond Shoals we lost sight of land, and I calmed down. Even though I wasn't at the wheel, I had the feeling of being in command, of my body, of my mind, of my own fate. I wasn't on that boat by chance. I felt the journey was part of a bigger design. I felt at home, as though I had returned to a familiar place.

During the two-hour run that took us beyond The Point off Hatteras, the mate spent his time filing very large hooks and cutting and coiling wire leaders to be attached to the monofilament with a snap swivel—the ball-bearing swivel that is indispensable for avoiding a twisted line. The rest of the time he rigged baits while I, a novice-in-training again, tried not to miss the smallest detail. He appreciated my attention and undisguised interest in learning his craft. He didn't mind when I examined the baits: large ballyhoos, small squids, some eels, mullet, known in my country as *lisa*, and the largest Spanish mackerel I'd ever seen, two feet long. Most fishermen I knew at the time would have been thrilled to catch any fish that size, never thinking of such a large creature as potential bait. The hook sizes were numbered from six to twelve, except the one for the mackerel, which was referred to as the "blue marlin hook." It was huge, the throat of the hook almost as wide as the palm of my hand.

All the baits and hooks with wire leaders of different strengths and lengths, set to entice the various species, had been properly rigged before we arrived at the fishing grounds. Five or six other boats were running at the same heading, and all but one—soon lost on the southeastern horizon—stopped in the same area. They all turned and started trolling in a following sea. Our captain detached and opened the outriggers from the flying bridge, extending them to each side of the boat. Those two large aluminum poles, thirty- to forty-feet long and attached to the sides of the boat, obliquely now at a forty-five-degree angle, are primarily used to separate the fishing lines when clipped to the release pins, these being attached to the halyard lines.

Holding the rod and reel, the captain asked the mate to attach the biggest rigged bait to the line he had lowered from the bridge. When the wired bait was attached to the snap swivel, the mate threw the bait into the ocean, to be controlled by the big reel the captain kept in a rod holder on the flying bridge's rail. Before that, the mate had attached smaller baits to six additional rods. These he placed in the water one by one, letting the farthest bait from the boat go first and then the middle ones, four being attached to the pins in the outriggers that, lifted with the halyards, would then be kept apart while skipping on the water well behind the boat. Then, the mate let go the last two: the flat lines, so called for being kept low from a pin in each corner of the transom, extended parallel to the water and trolled very close to the boat. In total, we had seven tempting baits on display.

Standing on the cockpit, I did not miss a single detail. "I can do the same!" I thought.

As soon as the big plastic teaser was tossed by the mate to one side of the wake, we had our first strike.

From that first day, I distinctly recall one particular sound: the fishing line that had been pressed by the wooden pin in the long left rigger came down with a crack. That sound, produced by the pin as the line is released, has to be the most gratifying musical note to the offshore fisherman's ear, together with the scream of the reel. Like my first ice cream, first Coca-Cola, and first love, that striking sound will be there, deep in my brain, until the end of my life.

The line raced rapidly from the spool, and, equally quick, the reel screamed for its loss. The faster the line, the louder the reel, as if they were rehearsing a harmonious drill. I couldn't understand what the captain was saying, apparently to me first, and then to the mate, but by instinct, I knew what to do.

I didn't lose time grabbing the rod. Whatever was fighting at the end of my line couldn't be the twin sister of that 600-pound huge blue marlin that I was hoping to catch. Though the pull was heavy, clearly it wasn't a giant fish. As soon as it jumped out of the water, I saw that it definitely was not what I had come to catch. It was my first mahimahi. Though I was accustomed to flounder, bluefish, and red and black drums, among other species, the mahimahi most resembled the other dorado, the great fighter I used to catch trolling in the Uruguay River.

As impressed as I once had been with my first dorado, I was equally amazed at the strength of this mahimahi at the end of my fishing line. Its characteristic squarish head and the slightly rounded angle of its forehead gave a fiery look to its unfriendly and defiant macho face. Hard to subdue, still feisty on the boat, mahimahis are capable of creating cockpit havoc. This mahimahi seemed large on deck; later on, the needle on the rusted scale at the dock would declare it to be slightly over fifty-two pounds, while the largest female I had caught that day was twenty-nine.

This was a good start, but the day was growing noticeably older by the hour without a hint of the dream fish I had come to chase. Several times the baits were attacked by smaller mahimahi. At other times there were yellowfin tunas, four or five of them, each around sixty pounds, but no blue marlin on the baits.

Around noon, I understood the mate to say something

like "We have plenty of time; there will be other strikes," while handing me a sandwich he had prepared with fresh mahimahi he had caught the previous day.

After lunch, he showed me the mechanical sequence of handling the rod, while introducing the concepts of free spool and drop back, "but only for marlin," he remarked.

"Free spool and drop back, only for marlin," I repeated. "But how will I know?"

"You'll see them, most of the time."

He was right. On subsequent trips, I would see the dark-brown shadow of a marlin underneath the trolled bait. Other times, out of nowhere, I would see—surging or appearing just behind the bait—six to eight inches of a tall, dark dorsal fin protruding out of the water, advancing erratically, slicing the sea like the thin blade of a circular saw.

With time I learned that it is a different bite when the marlin strikes. Unlike tuna—whose smoking gun is the white splash that it leaves at the bait site without jumping— the marlin, once hooked, will jump out of the water most of the time. But even when the marlin sounds, its pull will be strong but smooth compared with the accelerating, faster, longer, and deeper run of the tuna. Tunas always fight deep. After a while, the line will be almost vertical to the bottom, and every tuna will jerk the line several times in its attempt to escape.

With years of experience, I would learn that the white

marlin is a skilled predator, a thief with a threatening bill. The leery one of his clan, he's the one that rises to the bait but does not always strike and, when he does, is most tricky to catch. Like a baseball pitcher with a variety of pitches at various speeds, the white marlin has as many bites as he has speeds in his attack. If the free-spool drop back of the bait is too short as a consequence of prematurely engaging the reel, you will pull the bait out of its mouth and the marlin will be gone. *Adios!* Give him too much time to eat and he will oblige, eating the bait but leaving the ballyhoo head still attached to the hook. This is the white's signature card, its way of saying, "See ya next time." White marlin are master escape artists, often willing to teach you a new lesson, which, if compiled and learned, will give you, the angler, an advantage to outsmarting him the next time around. Or the next. Or the next.

A white marlin sometimes window-shops—looking, leaving, and then coming back to look one more time at different baits. Looking and buying, though, are two different things.

The marlin loves to go after a teaser, I think, because teasers are bigger, with presumably more food to eat, as in a daisy chain with its five or six plastic squids on line, nine to twelve inches a piece, and no hook in them. But swimming behind a teaser—or in pursuit of naturally rigged bait—doesn't equal a strike. The white marlin will tease you by making you think it will strike a particular bait, and, of

course, you'll lift that particular rod to no avail, for the marlin won't be munching that particular bait. It's not ready to
bite yet, if it ever will be. False alarm! In a flash, it may
switch to the short rigger bait just to inspect the offering,
then slide down to the long rigger bait and come forward
again, crossing the wake toward the other flat line. Many a
time I've run back and forth, alone on my boat, starboard to
port, as a white marlin pulls down from the pin one, two, or
even three lines, hitting the baits but keeping none, as I
keep lifting the right rod, only seconds behind, at the wrong
time. Will it ever take the bait? Hard to say. Sometimes the
marlin will disappear. Gone forever, one thinks. But there!
There! It's back. It's back right behind the bait. Amigo, be
patient. It's only a matter of time.

Are all billfish bites alike? Not at all. The strike of a
white marlin is distinct. You have to drop back only after it
touches the bait, otherwise the white will spook. However,
its cousin, the sailfish, will turn around and pick up the bait
in that case. Usually, the sail requires more drop-back time
before locking the reel and setting the hook. On the other
hand, the blue marlin, once zeroed in on the bait, seems
more determined to eat. It will charge and engulf the bait.
Sails and blues, to me, are much easier to entice to strike
and, then, much easier to hook up than whites.

A loud "pop" broke almost two hours of lull. For the tenth
time, a rigger line came down, but, unlike before, it wasn't

followed by the lamenting shriek of an engaged reel losing its line. Quickly, I lifted the rod while the bait continued skipping on the surface, apparently untouched.

But not for long. "Marlin!" the captain shouted.

As I had done with the practice rod earlier under the attentive eye of the mate, I followed the steps I thought I had learned: lift the rod from the rod holder, point the tip to the side at a ninety-degree angle, put your thumb on the line, free the spool, retracting the lever on the right side of the reel, and be ready for the drop back.

"Drop back!" came the order from the captain as the fish took the bait.

"Drop back!" echoed the mate.

Not once but twice I heard the order, but it went against all I knew to give away what somebody else wanted to take by force. Instinct prevailed over reason, and, contrary to their advice, I jerked back my rod as soon as I closed the drag. The bait flew forward. The marlin was left with an open, hungry mouth. Both captain and mate were distraught. I realized my mistake. But it was too late.

Except for my heart, pumping loud and fast, I was petrified, unable to move for a moment. The mate took another rod in his hands while the captain turned the boat around in a tight circle. Both men ignored me as they looked back, intently, over the boat's wake, expecting the marlin to resurface behind one of the baits.

We circled the area a couple of times, all eyes scanning

the strike zone. The mate brought in his bait and ordered me to reel in mine as well, though I still had it skipping—wounded, perhaps, from the bite, fifty yards from the stern. The boat was trolling again in a following sea. The excitement created by the aborted strike had gone out of the mate's eyes as if he'd given up hope; his tense body had relaxed, and his whole attitude had obviously changed. I suppose he thought me a novice—and I was. I felt bad, and it showed. However, the captain above and the mate by my side were soon composed, apparently resigned to the lost opportunity.

As I turned the handle of the reel a couple of times to bring in the bait, half-listening to the crew, half-talking to myself, I realized something was again trying to get behind my bait. I felt a strong "tap" in the thumb guiding the line into the reel. The rest of my left hand, holding the back fore grip of my rod, felt a second stronger tap and a pull. The unexpected touches accelerated my heartbeat. There followed an authoritative pull, and off went my line in a silent drop back in free spool. This time I was mentally prepared to let the unseen fish take my bait by force.

"Reel in! Reel in!" shouted the mate, thinking perhaps that I had not understood his instructions: he wanted to inspect the bait. Confused by the change in my posture and the line going out, he merely gestured, moving his closed right hand in vertical circles "waist high" as he grabbed and turned an imaginary handle of an invisible reel.

"Bring it in! The fish is gone," he called, unaware that something was taking my bait.

Although I was unable to see the prey running with the ballyhoo, I felt the speed of the line increase as it silently left the reel.

Before the mate could say more, the captain on the bridge noticed what was going on. With unthinking eloquence, he updated the mate, shouting in grammatically perfect patois: "Feeeiiisssssshhhh!"

"Feeiish?" called the mate in a high-pitched tone. "Same fish?"

"Lock it up! Lock it up!" thundered down the voice from the bridge. "Lock up the reel!" shouted the captain, a clear command to the angler-to-be and a heated response to the question asked by the mate.

I engaged the drag; immediately the line became tight, threatening to pull the rod from my hands. But holding it firm, I struck like the novice I was at big game—hard, as if I were mad at the fish and my purpose was to break the thumb-thick rod in two. Finesse wasn't yet part of my off-shore fishing repertoire. I was thinking of that 600-pound "blue" I had seen in the magazine.

The mate and the captain called out at once, "Fish on!" and "Hooked up!" with what I thought was some surprise. The rod had sustained the blow and was now bowing to the strength of the leaping billfish at the end of my line.

"White marlin," said the captain.

My first, I thought.

The fish jumped several times, far off, 200, 250 yards from the boat. Then it "sounded," and, after a short while, we had an oceanic stalemate. Something seemed to go wrong. I could feel a change in the weight, a shift in the pull, then a dull, heavier tension that I couldn't explain, not being familiar with marlin.

The captain backed down the vessel, making it easier to bring the fish next to the boat. A smaller version of my six-month-old dream came closer and closer to the starboard side. Standing up by the transom, the mate quickly grabbed the wire leader connected to the swivel, this one already touching the tip of the rod. Hand over hand, he pulled the fish closer to the boat.

"Tail-wrapped!" came down the voice from the bridge.

And, contrary to what I was expecting, the fish showed us its tail first. I was surprised to see its head still submerged at the opposite end.

"It's a blue," said the mate, in a surprised tone. He turned the fish around and held it by its bill. "A small blue!"

The captain also seemed surprised. I couldn't understand what was happening. They had called it a white marlin. How then could a white marlin turn into a "blue"? Besides, this fish was no 600-pounder like the blue marlin shown in the magazine ad. It wasn't even 100 pounds—maybe 70 or 80, at most. That's what was running through my head when I realized that the fish wasn't moving.

Dragged backward to the boat, the fish had accidentally drowned. The mate now held it by its bill and, with the boat underway, he tried to revive the marlin by forcing water through its mouth and gills. Together we made a long and gallant effort, but unfortunately we failed to resuscitate him. The only intention had been to fight the fish, but it didn't work out that way. The initial elation caused by the hook up of my first blue didn't last. Its death made me feel dejected and deflated.

"Wasn't your fault," reassured the mate. But thirty years later, the memory still has a bittersweet taste.

We boated the fish at 3:00 P.M. and called it a day. No one mentioned the chance that was lost, all of us assuming that the one we ended up catching was the one I had missed minutes before. With the single engine roaring again, we had over two hours to get back to the beach. I was exhausted— not so much from fishing but more from guessing the meaning of every word spoken to me.

Later, when we weighed the fish at the dock, the blue marlin barely weighed sixty-three pounds. "A rarity," the captain said, letting us know that it was the smallest blue ever caught on his boat.

Thirty years later, the fish hangs on the wall in my home in Annapolis. The names of the crew, as well as the name of the chartered boat, have slipped out of my memory, but I remember their faces, their gestures, their voices well. To this day, I wonder if the captain kept the picture that he took of that small trophy blue marlin suspended next to me, a big guy holding a thin rod with a comparatively small reel.

My first big-game lesson was, in a fashion, as successful as the one I had learned from my mother twenty-five years before.

FIVE

POOR MAN'S CANYON

MONDAY, AUGUST 5, 1996

The night before the first fishing day of the White Marlin Open, I had gone to sleep at midnight but woke before 4:00 A.M., without the benefit of an alarm clock. I had come to the conclusion that for the first day of fishing, my best chances of finding marlin would be to troll the waters around a site most captains and anglers call Poor Man's Canyon, a submerged ridge some 100 fathoms deep (about 600 feet) with a sloping bottom and several submerged natural bays. Accomack Canyon is the real name of this drop into the continental slope, and it is located some fifty-three nautical miles from the Ocean City sea buoy.

In the predawn hours, while brewing Salvadoran coffee

and toasting a bagel, I noted the offshore sea surface temperatures around the canyons, using the Rutgers University Sea Surface Temperature Chart that I had downloaded from the Internet. I figured that with a heading of 120 degrees, I'd probably have to travel between forty and sixty miles before arriving there and finding the right conditions to start trolling.

Outside, at 4:15, it was still dark. And quiet. The shadows seemed wrapped in solemn silence. I couldn't see a soul, and there was no sound from my boat's flags, inert wings cuddling their pole. Both the silence and the calm were good. I always like to be the first boat to leave the dock, especially when another 200 boats will be ready to depart at exactly 5:30 from the red sea buoy, one-half mile due east of the inlet. And I liked the composed, serene conditions that presaged even more calm later on.

I turned on *Caribeña*'s engines and broke the peace of the night. Then, running lights, radar, radio, depth finder, and Loran grid, all of them, seconds apart, came alive with blips, alarms, and winking lights. Going down to the cockpit, I knew I had all I needed for the journey ahead, but checked again; it's part of my routine before leaving the dock. So is checking that the transom light is really on, especially important since 199 boats will be behind us. I made sure that cooling water was flowing through the exhaust pipes, disconnected the electric cables, and took care of the transom, bow, and spring lines. Back on the bridge, I checked all the gauges on the dashboard of the boat. Every needle indicated that all the systems—oil pressure, water temperature in engines, battery charge—were working fine. With 350 gallons of fuel, we had twice the amount of diesel needed for an offshore fishing trip.

Reassured, I detached *Caribeña* from her moorings and pulled out from the slip. The sleepy harbor community began to recede behind us as we cruised at minimum speed through Harbor Island Marina toward its bottleneck head. Just as we were about to reach the open waters of the Isle of Wight Bay, I heard some people talking at the docks. I couldn't see a thing, but sensed that they were only yards away on my starboard side. A voice I failed to recognize called my name, wishing me luck. Without touching the wheel and keeping an eye on a narrow path that cut through the protruding bows of large boats in small slips, I acknowledged the greeting, "Thanks, amigo, and good luck to you!" As soon as we turned, my voice died on the air and the invisible man and the awakening marina were left behind.

The Kelly drawbridge, connecting the mainland to Ocean City over the Isle of Wight Bay, loomed a mile away. On the automatic one-watt channel 13 of my VHF radio, I alerted the attendant that I was on my way, approaching from the north. He promptly acknowledged. I kept an eye on the radar, which showed in its screen the west end of the city off my port beam, and the back-bay buoys and the large sandbar becoming an island off my starboard side. There was lots of water beyond, but only one safe channel to navigate for boats with *Caribeña*'s draft. Six knots felt like a snail's pace to me in the bridge, but at last I saw a massive structure of steel opening up before me, pivoting on its hinges. I cleared it in the dark and radioed the attendant: *"Caribeña* clear, Kelly Draw. Thanks for the lift!"

I increased speed; *Caribeña* needed more power to negotiate the strong swirls formed by the currents that rushed around the reinforced concrete pilings supporting the bridge. I passed the Coast Guard station and the final pier on the left and turned hard to port into the inlet that led from bay to open sea. Other boats were falling into line behind me, and hundreds of people stood up on the road by the north jetty, watching us depart.

Suddenly, this small corner of Ocean City looked like a city block of the downtown Buenos Aires I had known in my youth—bright with lights, full of life. The predawn crowd, the cars with their headlights, the city lights, the roaring of dozens of boat engines in front of the rocky seawall together created a level of excitement perfectly appropriate for the tournament's opening day.

At what was officially 5:30 sharp (although it said 5:34 on my wristwatch), a commanding voice on the VHF radio authorized the waiting boats to cross the imaginary sea-buoy line and depart.

The competition was on. The other captains and I brought our idling boats to a full run at exactly the same time, creating a thundering, deafening roar. A wave of boats and wakes began to flow away from shore, extending a mantle of foam over the unruffled seas. We were under way. It was exceptionally calm. No winds, no swells: a welcome change from the norm.

After a while, I could see in my radar where the fleet was heading. Three large, evenly divided groups had formed: one went toward Baltimore Canyon, a northeast course between 80 and 100 degrees; a second group, including *Caribeña*, headed 120 to 150 degrees toward Poor Man's Canyon and an undersea ridge known as the Rock Pile; and the third small fleet followed a course between 160 and 185 degrees, trying to reach the vicinity of Washington Canyon to the south and some undoubtedly going beyond, toward Norfolk Canyon.

If we were to draw a geometric figure of the tournament's fishing grounds, we would need to make a triangle, with its vertices resting on Ocean City, both lateral sides 85 miles long, one going northeast to the Wilmington Canyon and the other south to the Norfolk Canyon, with a 120-mile-long vertical line connecting these two canyons, some 80 miles offshore, parallel to the Delmarva Coast, where the ocean bottom is 6,000 feet down. I call this the Triangle of Hope, some 5,000 square miles, which is where we would look for marlin, or *aguja* in Spanish, which also means "needle." And properly so, since fishing for marlin in this huge portion of ocean is like trying to find the proverbial needle in a haystack.

The North American continental shelf—the underwater extension of the continental plain—was *above* the sea level 100,000 years ago. It was during that period that hardwood forests grew some 60, 100 miles off today's Virginia and New Jersey coasts. Today, this 35 to 100 mile–wide region of the mid-Atlantic between our present coasts and the offshore canyons is underwater again, and, unlike the deep ocean basins of the world formed by volcanic lava, the bottom of this shelf consists of deep deposits of sand, mud, and gravel, overlying crystalline rocks of vast thickness of consolidated sedimentary rocks. This underwater shelf slopes down some ten feet every mile until it reaches its offshore edge, called the shelf break. This break, or edge, runs parallel to the contour of the east coast of the United States.

The five major ocean canyons we fish today—Wilmington, Baltimore, Poor Man's, Washington, and Norfolk—were carved by ancient rivers during the periods of low sea levels produced by the glaciers, and their topography partially resembles the Grand Canyon of the Colorado River—layered, rocky, abrupt, and deep—but with only one wall, the west wall. At the other side of the shelf break is the continental slope to the abyss containing mountain ranges (ocean ridges), valleys, hills, and deep oceanic trenches, until it rises again in front of the African coast.

Normally, we fish at depths ranging from 40 to 1,000 fathoms, but most frequently we troll in and out and parallel to the shelf break, or crisscross the deep V-shaped canyons, where the comparatively gentle slope ends abruptly and the ocean bottom drops from 600 feet, to 1,200 and 2,000 feet a few hundred yards toward the east, continuing eastward to reach depths of 6,000 feet seventy or eighty miles from the coast.

The canyons, as much as the Gulf Stream itself, are corridors for pelagics like billfish and tunas who follow schools of bait fish—from mackerel to squid—which in turn feed on the plankton around the benthos originating the food chain. The oceanic currents and undercurrents collide with the submerged granite walls of the chasms stirring life . . . and death.

Today, this is the marlin's kingdom. But the levels of our four-billion-year-old oceans have always fluctuated by as much as 220 meters. One hundred million years ago a vast inland ocean covered almost all the land of the eastern seaboard, the southern states, and all the midwestern states. Marlin and swordfish, I guess, may have been at home on the "deep oceanic waters" off Missouri and Tennessee, roaming all over Utah and Wyoming, and running up and down the Grand Canyon, exactly as they do today over the great canyons off the continental shelf.

The boats in the tournament, like the billfish in recent weeks, would be scattered all over the ocean, some approach-

ing latitude 39° N, others farther south at around the 37°
latitudinal line. Few vessels, if any, would venture beyond
longitude 73° W. No one over the past weeks had found a
real hot spot or a steady bite in these waters. It was anybody's guess where *las agujas blancas* might be.

Of course, the fastest boats—those that can make thirty
knots, thirty-five knots, even more—could go and fish virtually any place they choose, 120, even 150, and still get in
plenty of fishing by the mandatory 3:30 P.M. quitting time.
With the engine power I have on *Caribeña*, however, I could
only travel 70 miles from Ocean City if I wanted to start fishing with the rest of the fleet by 8:30 A.M.

The unusually flat sea allowed me to cruise at twenty-
two knots, full of fuel, full of water, full of food, full of hope.
Even at that speed, in one hour I would have fallen some
three to ten miles behind a good half of the fleet going my
way. I would also be slightly to their north, since from the
outset of the run, I had positioned myself a few hundred
yards to the north of this collective eastern run, on a slightly
divergent course. I maintained this oblique heading for
twenty minutes or so, distanced myself sufficiently to avoid
the crowds, then struck out on a clear path to my destination. Experience is a wonderful tool.

The absence of wakes and a radar screen showing no
dots for a radius of a mile and a half confirmed an empty
ocean in front of *Caribeña*. Sixty or more fellow competitors
were running a parallel course a couple of miles ahead,

abeam, and abaft my boat—but all a couple of miles south of my starboard side. Three or four others were some miles to port. I was virtually running alone—nothing in front of me but the horizon; no boundaries, save those of my imagination; no speed limits; no one to respond to but myself. There's nowhere else on earth where I could feel such freedom and possess such wealth.

As always, the rising sun's first rays of light glowing orange struck me as awesome, humbling. I thought of my parents, for years now walking the serene paths of their Other Life. It's their warmth, as much as the sun's, that I felt in my soul. At sea, my parents, like playful dolphins, often seem to intercept my path and run alongside me.

Caribeña raced through the waves. My wristwatch confirmed what the now-yellow sun told me: two and a half hours had elapsed since departure. The sea surface temperature alarm sounded. We were coming across a temperature break and a weak, disseminated line of weeds. The thermometer jumped from 74.4 to 76 degrees. The depth finder said that *Caribeña* was floating on 70 fathoms, or 420 feet. Making a U-turn and heading back to the west for less than a quarter-mile, I saw the break—different colors in adjacent waters, scattered weeds, signifying an incoming current.

It was 8:15—fifteen minutes to tournament time. Barely drifting in the morning calm, I saw a boat coming to a halt just a quarter-mile to the south. Then another boat, with its outriggers opened like a bird stretching its wings, pulled up close to the first boat, ready to troll. A few more boats went by, then one doubled back. Yet another, on my port side a mile away, headed south toward me. At 8:30, I counted nine boats ready to fish. Twenty minutes earlier, I had been alone.

Osprey was one of the boats ready to fish, Captain Jim Drosey at the helm. I could see Anthony Williams at the cockpit. Williams was the owner of *The Elixir,* recently sold; he was fishing with the *Osprey* while a new *Elixir* was being built. The other member of the team looked like Al Bednarik. At a distance, we waved and exchanged greetings. I have known the trio for years. They have won so many times at so many different competitions that if this game were football, they would be Bill Walsh, Joe Montana, and Jerry Rice.

Seeing them reinforced my belief that I was in the right place. We had often roamed the same fishing grounds, witnessing one another's catch, finding similar success. In such a case, our fishing ground would become the Secret Spot, unknown to the majority of the fleet, especially those sideband talkers from Oregon Inlet to Cape May—radio jockeys who seemed to spend more time jawing than fishing. Of course, whatever happens at sea, whatever the subject, one way or another, it will always be discovered; it will always be revealed, like the whereabouts of ships lost at sea that even years or centuries later resurface with myriad details. Consider the saga of *Nuestra Señora de Atocha,* the Spanish galleon sunk in 1622, with forty tons of gold and silver and thirty *kilos de esmeraldas*, in the warm waters off the Florida Keys that was discovered by treasure-hunter Mel Fisher after a fifteen-year search around Marquesas Keys in 1985, or even the great tale of the *Titanic*, finally discovered in its icy tomb on the floor of the northern Atlantic. It is the same with marlin fishing: there are no secrets that can be kept for long. Sooner or later, tonight or before sunrise tomorrow, everybody would know what was going on, and where.

"Gentlemen, it's eight thirty. Lines in the water. The competition is on. Good luck!" the voice of the committee boat rang authoritatively through the VHF.

Eight thirty-four by my wristwatch. The first day of competition in the 23rd White Marlin Open Tournament. One hundred ninety-eight out of the 237 participant boats began to troll over depths ranging from forty to more than a thousand fathoms in an enormous field of play. The 39 boats not fishing today were most likely kept at the docks expecting to see if and where the marlin would be caught by the fleet. More or less in the middle of that field, I engaged *Caribeña*'s 3208 Cats, as these engines are known, setting a course south by southeast bordering the thicker patches of the pelagic seaweed. The absence of wind and the tame waters made the Atlantic look like a gigantic lake.

I kept the engines shy of the 800-rpm mark and trolled at 5.2 knots. The speed produces a harmonious h-u-u-u-m-m-m in the motors that reverberates through the hull. I like the sound, and I am convinced that the marlin is attracted to it or, anyhow, doesn't greatly object to it.

Soon I had five lines fishing; the gunwales bristled with rods, all upright and leaning toward the wake but tilted at different angles and paying out different lengths of line to offer bait at different points in the ocean. Two long riggers extended some 80 to 100 feet out; two short riggers, 30 to 35 feet; and a center line, like the middle spot on the five-face of dice, split the difference at about 45 to 50 feet. My habitual spread. No flat lines parallel to the water; everything was on a rigger—even the perennial teaser off the transom gunwale, next to the starboard side. The teaser, aimed simply at luring fish, not catching them, is a daisy chain of five, sometimes six, squid—no hooks. These are soft, medium-sized, bill-abused, amber-colored, plastic squid. They are independently attached to a fifty-pound line on a Penn International reel, seated on a twenty-year-old Fenwick rod fitted into the starboard rod holder.

I fished standing up on the cockpit. Every now and then—by design or simple impulse—I climbed to the bridge to check everything: first, always, the trolled baits, then the different gauges, an often-repeated check to confirm that the engines were working fine. Then I observed the surrounding waters, and, if any, the boats and the fleet—both live and on the radar screen. From that vantage point, I looked for skipping bait, jumping large fish, or telltale slicks (from bigger fish feeding on bait), floating birds, and weed lines or debris that could attract small fish and then larger ones in their wake.

But seldom do I spend time on the bridge. My war room is the cockpit. It was there that I had added a second set of engine controls. As a solo fisherman, I need them, first and most important, because in order to achieve my high rate of hook ups, I have to be able to reach and hold my rod in my hands before the fish even touches the bait. And, second, I need the extra controls to avoid going up and down the ladder when fighting the fish. They are on the slanted top of a cabinet under the ladder going to the bridge, on the port side—the heart of my operation—where I keep an automatic-pilot remote control that has a window showing my course, and a 1½-inch knob for steering. I also have a digital compass and a multifunction electronic device displaying basic readings for surface temperature, trolling speed, miles run, and depth. I normally stand next to this cabinet, my right hand closeby or on the knob of the automatic-pilot remote control. The other electronic controls are easily reachable, allowing me to operate everything with my right hand—even when my left hand is holding the rod with a fighting fish, however big, hooked at the end of the line.

The controls are important, but the reality is that I fish with my brain. I always try to be aware of where I am and what's nearby, from fishing markers to boats; where they are, how many there are, and, if moving, what their course or trolling patterns are. I also need to know where I'm going, so I can mentally adjust for any course alterations. The characteristics of the bottom structure below me, the depths of the spot and the surrounding areas I fish, are as important as the sea surface temperature and its possible breaks. I always set *Caribeña*'s alarms to let me know if there is a change of one degree or more of temperature, up or down.

I've been fishing these waters with my own boats for twenty-five years; I know the topography of the ocean floor here like I know my back. I know just where and how much the bottom declines the farther you go from shore. If I start trolling at a depth of 100 fathoms at the edge of Poor Man's Canyon, on a course of 120 degrees, in less than one mile, I will be fishing in 200-plus fathoms; a half hour later, the bottom will be 350 fathoms. One hour later, or five miles farther if I am moving at a speed of 5.2 knots, *Caribeña* will be over 600 fathoms—3,600 feet of ocean.

Obviously this tridimensional perception of the sea and knowing whatever is submerged at various depths comes with years of practical experience and reading depth finders and bathymetric charts, which show in amazing detail the various contours of the oceanic bottom. After a while, one recognizes specific islands, hills, and ravines. In a way, it is like an airplane pilot who is constantly aware of the space in front, underneath, and above his craft.

My depth finder is capable of reading down to 400 fathoms, or around 2,500 feet. Over that depth, when I need to be exact, I check a second Loran, mounted on top of the counter inside the cabin, and an area chart with overlying time-differential lines. Next to the Loran, I have a second VHF radio mounted on the cabin wall, this one primarily used to announce catch and releases in official events, answer incoming calls, or give information if somebody wants to know how I'm doing or where I am. Both the Loran (always turned on) and the VHF (often turned off) are reachable from the cockpit.

Caribeña, in terms of seaworthiness and strength, must be at the top of any boat list, but in a luxury sense is simple, rudimentary, even borderline Spartan. As a fishing machine, she lacks what most of the elegantly appointed sportfishing vessels in the tournament possess as a matter of course: no soaring tuna tower from which to keep a lookout over the seas, no fighting chair in which to sit with some comfort, feet braced, as you battle a marlin. She does not have those enormous two-speed reels mounted on thumb-thick rods with extra-wide roller guides and bent butts that look impressive when displayed from a fighting chair. Neither does *Caribeña* have a tuna door in the transom nor a gin pole, as they're called, with a pulley system that can raise a big fish into the boat—should one be needed. She lacks sophisticated, commercial-fishing electronics and underwater cameras. Her hull is not stenciled with tuna and squid images that many believe attract fish close to the boat and its baits. There is no cellular phone on board with unlimited range, no Global

Positioning System, no single side band radio to reach boats faraway or people on shore. There is no raft, nor is there an EPIRB (Emergency Position Indicating Radio Beacon) to transmit our location to the satellites orbiting earth in the extreme case that I have to abandon ship. These two items aren't required by law. But I do have the mandatory gun and emergency flares and three radios on board. These, in sum, are *Caribeña*'s haves and have-nots among at least another dozen supposedly essential items.

But then, there might be one or more reasons for not having one, some, or most of these supposedly essential items. Perhaps they are not that important. Perhaps they are overrated. I certainly can't afford some of them, and, in fact, if I could, the size of the crew aboard *Caribeña* would make it virtually impossible to use all those gadgets. Nor is there sufficient evidence to conclude that I would be a better angler or a more successful sportsman if I had them on board.

Could I possibly win the tournament without all those accoutrements? By week's end, we would know.

Osprey, early in the morning, fishing close by, hooked up with a back-breaking fish. Tony Williams, a great guy in a small frame who might weigh less than 140 pounds but has a knack for big fish, was fighting a bigeye tuna estimated over 200 pounds that could pull him overboard, but, accustomed to catching blue marlin of 600 or 700 pounds, he and his crew gaffed and boated the bigeye before noon. (This

tuna would win first prize in the tournament, weighing in at
235.5 pounds.)

Except for that action and a few scattered billfish raised—
perhaps half of them hooked and released—nothing else
happened during the morning of opening day. Weather-wise
it was a delightful day, but a day of futile hunting for most
boats. On *Caribeña* I didn't have a single strike, not even a
mahimahi, so common in these seas. And according to several broadcasts on different channels of the VHF, that was
the norm. What little action there was on billfish appeared
to have been to the south of Poor Man's Canyon, below the
Rock Pile, above Washington Canyon, around the 41900
line on the Loran, in sixty fathoms of water. As is so often
the case in fishing, the action almost always occurs a few
miles away from where you are.

I was not discouraged. I had been at this game a long
time. In fact, I was getting old at it. I trolled. I thought. I observed: the sea, its temperatures, the depths. I watched and
checked the baits. I thought a little more. I was now com-
mitted to an inshore search at depths of less than fifty fathoms. Nothing scientific. Just a hunch. Perhaps the action
was inside the break. Although the water was greenish—
and green waters, we believe, normally have fewer marlin—
it seemed to have more life there, with some natural bait
and the occasional birds looking for food.

On the table-flat sea, time dwindled away on the rare
calm of afternoon—and nibbled at my hopes of a marlin

strike. Soon it would be the end of the fishing day. One more time, I changed the untouched baits. Five naked ballyhoos—my usual spread.

This time it worked. The dark, rounded, and unmistakable dorsal fin of a white marlin broke the afternoon lull, slicing in two the tiny, narrow wake left by the trolled ballyhoo on the starboard side. I jumped to the rod. A second later, it was ready in my hands. I pointed its tip to the fish. The white marlin broke the surface, closing the gap between itself and the bait. I could see its dull colors changing into bright hues of electric blue as it took the bait in its mouth. I dropped back the bait, lifting my thumb off the line to free it. The boat went forward, and the bait and fish stayed in the same place, as the line of my reel flowed out in free spool, allowing the marling to mangle the bait in its jaws. I paused. The line fled from the reel. Intuition, instinct, vibrations, changes of speed in rapid succession prompted my counterattack.

Now. I engaged the reel, and the line tensed. I saluted the marlin in two, three hard jerks on the rod. The rod bent, and the fish, as if caught by surprise, leapt into the air.

It was a solid hook up. The fight took seven minutes. I struggled the fish to the transom and port corner and grabbed the swivel connecting leader and line. I tagged the fish and earned an extra five points.

It wasn't just the points that made me want to tag the fish; I do it as a matter of principle. Tagged fish are tracked throughout the world's oceans; the tagging thus yields important information about the marlin's migratory habits, spawning grounds, rate of growth, and life span.

In 1955, the Ocean City Light Tackle Club, with the Woods Hole Oceanographic Institution, initiated a tagging program at Ocean City. This was the first time a major sportfish-tagging research study had ever been undertaken, and its results have provided new and fascinating information: the life span of the white marlin is known to be ten to twelve years—longer than it was once thought to be. It has definitely been proven that these fish readily survive the shock of being caught, tagged, and released (records indicate that bleeding fish, fish that have expelled their stomachs, and fish with damaged fins or tails have survived and been recaptured), and some migration routes have been established.

The majority of tags have been placed by sportfishermen. Since the program's inception in 1954 through the end of 1997 (the last time the results were compiled), 30,408 white marlin have been tagged. There have been 522 recoveries of tags by anglers and long-liners.

Most whites have been recaptured in the same area where they were tagged, often years later. One, tagged off Ocean City by one of our members in 1980, was recovered by an angler 1,458 days later, off Ocean City. La Guaira, Venezuela, has been the setting for a couple of spectacular recoveries: a white tagged there in 1984 was recovered there six years later. In 1993, another white was recaptured at La Guaira that had been tagged there nine years earlier.

Through the tags, we have discovered that many marlin are travelers. One fish swam 5,000 kilometers from the Bahamas, where it was tagged, to the waters off the mouth of the Amazon River, where it was recovered. In 1984, a fish tagged and released off the southern coast of the Dominican Republic was recaptured about 570 miles east of Atlantic City, New Jersey, forty-three days later. In 1985, a white marlin that had been tagged at Bimini on June 1, 1978, was recovered at La Guaira, Venezuela, after having been at liberty for 2,499 days—approximately six years.

The all-time record for time at large, almost twelve years, was set by a white caught forty miles south of Block Island in July 1982. It had been tagged by Ann and Kim Yellott off Ocean City on September 26, 1970. Upon its recovery, the fish was reported to be in "shabby" condition, and the tag was so completely encrusted by marine growth that it was barely recognizable as a "tag."

Nineteen ninety-two saw the recapture of a white marlin more than nine years after it was tagged. It was released off Grand Isle, Louisiana, and was recovered off Virginia Beach, Virginia. It had gained only an estimated fifteen pounds in the interim. Others aren't that lucky being that many years at large, or gaining only a few pounds, or finding a glorious, sportive end: In 1985, there was one of the most unusual recaptures in the history of the Cooperative Gamefish Tagging Program when a commercial U.S. long-liner that was retrieving his longline discovered two consecutive hooks had only the heads of white marlins attached. On the next hook was a mako shark, which, when it was gutted, contained the torso of a white marlin that had a tag embedded in the flesh. This fish had been tagged in Norfolk Canyon four years earlier.

In 1995, a white tagged at Cozumel was caught in the central Atlantic 286 days later, a distance of 2,482 nautical miles. In 1992, a white tagged in January 1991, at St. Thomas, Virgin Islands, was recaptured in August 1992, by a local drift fisherman off Morocco, the first documented transatlantic crossing by a white marlin, an oceanic traverse of 3,150 nautical miles.

Blue marlin also travel. One tagged off Charleston, South Carolina, in May 1992, was recovered below the equator 500 miles east of Natal, Brazil. Another tagged in the Wilmington Canyon (off New Jersey's coast) was recaptured off the Indian Ocean island of Mauritius in 1992. The minimum distance it could have traveled was 9,100 nautical miles—a long-distance record for any fish. In the forty-year history of the tagging program, it was the first fish of any species to demonstrate movement out of the Atlantic and its adjacent seas into another ocean.

It is not now known whether the white marlin found in the Caribbean, the Gulf of Mexico, and off the Mid-Atlantic

Bight are one stock or different stocks. There has been a number of tag returns which suggest some intermixing of the fish found in these areas. One, a fish tagged at Ocean City on August 8, 1988, by one of our OCLTC members, was recovered a year later from the Gulf, about fifty miles south of Mobile, Alabama. The 1991 and 1992 tag returns show some minimal trading of whites between the mid-Atlantic area and the Caribbean and Gulf of Mexico, but the majority are still recaptured in the areas where they were tagged.

I tagged my fish. Not bad for a remarkably slow day. I had one more task before I released the marlin, one that did not involve earning extra points but just satisfaction. Holding the leader with my left hand, I picked up the camera, aimed, and shot several times, photographing the catch, its tag, and the number 237, *Caribeña*'s official identification in the tournament. The tournament works on the honor system: you don't need to prove you've caught your fish—your word is good.

Finally, I was ready to show some compassion toward the beaten fish, whose weight couldn't have exceeded fifty-five pounds. Grabbing it by its bill, I twisted free my number 5 Mustad hook from its upper jaw, and let him go.

I rinsed my hands, checked my wristwatch, deducted four minutes from the actual time, called the committee boat, and announced, as required, that Boat 237 had just tagged and released a white marlin. It gave me the official time—1:47 P.M. I was on the board with seventy-five points.

That was it for the day. I showed my inverted white marlin flag as I returned to the dock, letting everyone know I had released a billfish. It didn't look like a lot. But 198 boats had caught only thirty-seven white marlin that day.

SIX

•

•

THE QUEEN AND I

The first time I laid eyes on her was in the spring of 1984. She was on the other side of the deep creek, charming and graceful against a background of blossoming dogwoods and old weeping willows, swaying provocatively with the southerly winds of spring. I noticed the dark-blue detail lines around her deckhouse and fly bridge that showed off her shapely lines and contrasted with the taut white fiber of her skin. She looked very young. I was young at heart; and both of us were in excellent shape.

By contrast, at this other side of the canal was the end of a six-year relationship that was . . . OK, but no more than that. It never was real love. It was more infatuation and compromise. It was dwindling to a friendly breakup, leaving me free to move on with the winds and the tides.

Six years before, we had both been first-timers with so much to learn from the sea. From the very beginning we had an implicit agreement: we would *try*. But eventually we arrived at the inevitable: it was time to change our courses and sail apart. As with any relationship, ours was hard to give up. There was a sense of loss and the unavoidable sadness that many *adios* bring. But as dreadful as it can be to start all over again, sometimes it's the only way to move on in life. I had regrets, but not many. My two marriages had not lasted, and I was not as close to my daughter as I would have liked to be.

I knew it would be hard to match the beauty of my first boat's woodwork. Her cabinetry and railings showed the craftsmanship typical of Egg Harbor boats. But she simply was not capable of getting me where I wanted to go. It was a point in my life when I wanted to search for the uncommon, the outstanding, the best—to see what challenges were to be found in the depths of more distant canyons, to wander far from shore for long lengths of time. My under-powered thirty-three-foot *Pica Olas* (Wave Breaker) simply wasn't up to the task.

Caribeña, on the other hand, did not have *Pica Olas*'s beauty or degree of refinement, but I knew in advance that she had range and superior strength to take me to the off-shore canyons and beyond. And she had better command on rough seas that would amply compensate for her hard edges and lack of interior glamour. I couldn't stop admiring her;

she was definitely my "chosen one," even when she was already engaged—taken, owned, out of reach, kept at bay, securely tied. And then, early one fall morning, she was gone.

If inconspicuous had been her arrival, equally surreptitious was her disappearance. It left behind for me, at the dock, an enormous, empty space. And there was no clear indication that she would ever come back.

·

·

·

I sold *Pica Olas* that fall and became boatless as winter descended. Almost a year went by, until somebody who knew me from the marina told me that she was available, waiting for someone to take good care of her.

It turned out she was in Florida. Her owner, John Ford, had bought a bigger boat: a Bertram 42'. She was indeed on the market. I wanted to see her at once, face-to-face.

Raymond Curry, a gracious and knowledgeable man well familiarized with Bertram boats, picked me up at the airport. He took me to a commodious waterfront house, on the canals of Ft. Lauderdale, owned by the dealer who was handling *Caribeña*'s sale.

I looked her over closely. She was in excellent shape. We went out, and I tested the power of her twin Cats in a sea trial. I liked the way she ran, turned, and stopped. I enjoyed the tone of her engines. She danced well with the waves. Backing down on an imaginary marlin, she was assertive and swift, even though she wasn't outfitted for fishing; she had been strictly a pleasure boat, given to cruising. I made up my mind to buy her, but I did not yet make an offer. The asking price was $165,000. I flew back to Washington and made a counteroffer, which was accepted. I was back afloat.

She had been the *Irish Rover*, but I re-christened her *Caribeña*. *Cari be ña*. *Cari*, pronounced like in *Chari*-sma, *be* like in *be*-st and *nia*, like in Pennsylva-*nia* (*Chari-be-nia*), which means "Caribbean Girl."

Before leaving Florida, *Caribeña* was rigged for serious off-shore fishing—to the tune of $12,000—with the addition of Lee's outriggers and rod holders and new Raytheon electronics. A new interior—including curtains, upholstery, and starboard-to-port carpet—would be completed when she arrived in Annapolis.

I brought her up from Florida myself with a mate familiarized with Bertram boats for the first leg of the trip through the inland waterway. It included an overnight stop in Jacksonville. I don't generally like the waterway—I find it too confined; there are drawbridges, and you can't go at full speed all the time. Ten miles offshore you have all the water in the world. But I think many people are, perhaps, afraid of the open ocean. From Jacksonville, I went on to Morehead City, and Hatteras on the open sea, getting a feel for my new boat. After that last port of call, I kept her for over a month at the fishing center in Nags Head, North Carolina.

I had fished those offshore waters before and wanted to hire a knowledgeable local captain to allow me to concentrate in the cockpit. Dick Bailey, who often used to fish from chartered boats at that time, recommended that I hire a man named Bill Hogan. Bill had just the disposition I was looking for. A local man, he was willing to come aboard and share what he knew about the shifting channels and the treacherous waters of the Outer Banks, where a yard off course can mean your boat will be left high and dry on a sandbar.

A quiet and unassuming man, Bill also knew how to rig baits. Being the mate by default on my own boat, I watched whatever he did, and whatever I knew about boat handling and fishing was greatly improved by his skill. Fishing methods, like languages, are in constant flux, and while I assimilate changes rather slowly, I do adopt them eventually.

Innovations take time to grow roots. Some never succeed. The basics remain. Thirty years ago everyone fished with squid, but nowadays other baits prevail. But I still sometimes rig squid, for variety and a certain almost mystical charm they have for me. And I rig them in the same way I rigged thirty years ago.

During those weeks in Nags Head, *Caribeña* and I caught plenty of tuna, mahimahi, and billfish with Bill Hogan at the helm, including a 350-pound blue marlin, which I tagged and released.

The blue engulfed a 15-pound mahimahi, being reeled in by a guest of my friends Jack and Marion McDonald aboard my boat. When Mr. Smith, an executive-turned-lucky-first-time-big-game-angler, told the story six months later during a Christmas party at the McDonalds' house, the blue had grown to 600 pounds. A year later, same place, similar party, *almost* same story, the marlin, in jest, was "a 1,000-pounder." Who knows how much it weighs today!

But, jokes aside, it was during this period beyond Diamond Shoals that *Caribeña* showed her serious side, the legendary Bertram stuff on the turf of legendary boats. Bertram introduced the innovative deep-V design of its hulls in its famously acclaimed 31 footers, and then transferred this design to the Bertram 35s. Having fished from Bertrams 28, 31, 35, 37, 38, 42, 43, 46, 50, and 54, I give kudos to the very comfortable ride of the 50 and its spacious cockpit, but I personally think (unbiased, of course) that the latest 35 is the boat I prefer for my kind of fishing—a medium-weight with the punch and the chin of a heavyweight. *Caribeña* has proved, time and again, that she can take big seas and high winds.

She and I would face tests that would push our courage and endurance to the limit. And in those experiences I would start to feel the deep bond that leads captains to go down with their ships. But that was yet to come. In 1985, I was immensely proud of *Caribeña* as she rode bow to bow with the big boys of the Oregon Inlet Charter Fleet. Those were the days of Captain Ommi Tillet's *The Sportman* and Captain Harry Baum's *Jo Boy*, whose fishing accomplishments are well known. Tillet was one of the pioneer boat builders in the region and an excellent captain, and Baum and his boat were the first to catch a "grander," a blue marlin weighing more than 1,000 pounds. Had this sport been golf, their achievements could be compared with those of Arnold Palmer and Jack Nicklaus, although the size of a golf ball may be five times smaller than a blue marlin's eyes.

Caribeña and I have made a nice couple. For better or worse: on sickening days of high winds and furious seas or on windless days of gently rolling waves; on successful fishing days when we catch and release billfish; or on those days when we got skunked.

I have no doubt that she will keep me afloat, reach faraway fishing spots, raise marlin, and play them fairly from the square stern. We may keep losing one now and then, but we learn from our losses to do better next time around.

•

•

•

Caribeña's motto could have been "Fearless Fishing for Fun" in those first years with her when I was still an apprentice to the sea and its marlin. I had to learn (the hard way, of course) that true success in offshore fishing does not come from inverted marlin flags and spectacular fights. It is accomplished when you are securely tied at the dock after a safe return from the deep.

In the late 1980s, on one of those rare occasions when fishing with friends, I was sixty-eight miles off the Maryland shore with Rum Maddox, then seventy-five, and his much younger nephew Tom Maddox. *Caribeña* and I had moved beyond the initial first flush of our relationship and had started to test its limits.

It was an uneventful day with one white marlin caught and released by Tom. When it was time to come home, *Caribeña*'s steering didn't respond. No way could I make her turn. And with reason: she had lost her two rudders to electrolysis, a chemical change in metal that softens it until it disintegrates. One rudder may have been lost on the way out to the canyon. It had felt peculiar to steer the boat in the strong current under the drawbridge over one of Ocean City's back bays, and later, on the way out to the fishing grounds. I remember stopping a couple times to check the hydraulic system, the pressurized air, and its tiller arm, trying to find something wrong, but everything looked fine this side of the hull.

The second rudder had probably snapped from its post under the pressure exerted by tons of water *Caribeña* had turned during the marlin fight at the end of the day. We had released an average white marlin that, being foul hooked, gave us a fitting fight, but we paid what seemed a big price when we lost the only rudder left to steer us home. We were a mere sixty-eight nautical miles from the Ocean City sea buoy, going in circles, thinking that my trust in bronze had sunk with the last rudder to the bottom of the sea. However, having twin engines and a pair of reliable trim tabs to stabilize and even change our course with proper manipulation brought peace of mind to the crew during the four-hour run home.

That day, in 1985, was the first time that I had lost both rudders of my boat. But it wouldn't be the last. They were replaced with identical twins, but, like their sisters, the new bronze rudders were destined to live short lives. Electrolysis would strike again. And again, of course, it would happen far from shore, in the deep Atlantic, though this second occasion I was alone. At least that time I didn't have to worry about having concerned friends on board.

Like the first time, I came back steering with the twin engines and the trim tabs. Once on land, I learned that there were no rudders shelved anywhere in stock to readily replace those I had lost. They would have to be ordered and would take at least three weeks to arrive from Florida, for the manufacturer was starting summer vacation the same day I called. I thought my fishing season was over until another member of the Ocean City Marlin Club, George McNab, offered to help.

"Same thing happened to my thirty-five," he said, fishing now from his new Bertram 50', *Reel Machine*. George was also the owner of a machine shop, fabricating all kinds of metal parts, from kneecaps and hip joints to highly specialized avionics parts, and he was more than capable of making a set of rudders for my boat. I was impressed. "We only need the blueprint of the rudders," he said. "The computer will do the rest." What George didn't say was that he was also filling commercial orders for thousands of parts that were far more important than mine. Only a fellow fisherman would know how important it was to have my boat fixed in the three or four weeks before the marlin migrated south.

George fashioned two massive blocks of stainless steel. "When they're finished," he said, "they will be immune to electrolysis."

While my rudders were being manufactured, there was a tournament organized by the Ocean City Marlin Club. Since I was rudder-less, everyone assumed that I wouldn't compete. Imagine George's surprise when trolling in *Reel Machine* in the canyons sixty miles offshore he spotted *Caribeña* 200 yards abeam his starboard side.

From the cockpit he talked to his captain on the fly bridge, gesturing and pointing, seemingly asking to approach my boat. Closer, leaning against the gunwale of his own vessel, he seemed to say "how come," with his arms high in the air, extended apart, with an incredulous question mark on his face. He was evidently surprised, and now knowing him better, I guess he was making an effort not to look annoyed. He couldn't believe his eyes. Nowadays he really laughs, shaking his head like he did then, in disbelief, when he relates the story to those who gather at the dock on those windy or stormy days that keep us on land. That tournament day, once he realized that I was indeed the one on the boat waving back at him, he was thinking of the stainless steel rudders he was still manufacturing for me, and there I was, rather rudely riding alongside, "obviously with a 'new' pair of rudders" that probably Bertram Yachts, from Florida, found, sold, and surely sent to me overnight through UPS! How could I have done something like that! He called me on the VHF. And gently, as a gentleman that he really is, asked how I was doing. It took me a while to convince him that at the last minute I had decided to participate in the tournament and go out to fish . . . without rudders!

Going out was OK, although I have to say that I really wanted to go to the Washington Canyon, but I found that the moderate early morning winds from the south were more persuasive than I had anticipated. After a while, it was obvious to me that, while any canyon would make a fine destination, circumstantial Poor Man's Canyon was the best choice.

Caribeña and I finally reached the new ideal depth of fifty fathoms, and we were ready to troll. But without rudders, I was unable to turn her around at will. At only five knots, I was constantly pushed hither and yon by capricious waves and uncooperative winds that tested my patience and handicapped seamanship skills. We caught nothing, and I had to stop and correct my course several times during the three-hour-plus run back. And while I had a good time challenged by the new experience at sea, I unwittingly had made family and friends worry until they saw *Caribeña* returning to the safety of my dock. Borrowing a phrase from a senior member of the 55th Congress of the United States of America: "It was an indiscretion of my youth," even if I was over forty-two.

·

·

·

These experiences forged a closeness and connection between me and *Caribeña*. But my true bonding with *Caribeña* came with storms. It was in the roughest seas that I really learned to trust my boat, because, literally, my life was in her hands.

There have been many times during the hunt when I have found myself assailed by unexpectedly unfriendly seas. Terrible was the sudden awareness that I was at the corner of "Dangerous Spot" and "Save Me, God!" ambushed by a furtive storm, battered by a violent squall which, like a deranged puppeteer who used magic instead of thread, jostled *Caribeña* up and down like a marionette.

I remember one particular storm late in the summer of 1992. The weather offshore had been clear, hot, humid, and calm. That morning, I caught and released two white marlin. Then the action ceased, so I gauged that I had come in at the tail of the bite. I decided to linger offshore a couple more hours, on a southerly course, hoping to find a new bite that afternoon. Light winds from the south pushed me closer to a two-knot ascending current, rife with sargasso weeds that I had heard about earlier on the radio from boats fishing south of me. Warmer water and weeds, of course, meant the chance of more bites.

I hadn't anticipated, though, that the wind would switch to the west and pick up speed. For hours before—unbeknownst to me—a roaring squall had been gathering force and was rushing to intercept our path. The first inkling of trouble was a blackening sky, coming in low and fast out of the northwest. A sea that minutes before had been blue tinged almost instantly turned slate gray. Suddenly, the breeze became a wind, and the wind turned into a gale; the outriggers' halyards howled, and the crests of the waves rose like the heads of cobras.

Alone at the helm, I did not even dare think that I was in control. I knew better. I just wanted to keep an eye—the sharpest eye—on those six-, eight-, ten-foot waves that we first had to climb before worrying about plummeting down the slopes of their far sides into the bottom of the troughs.

One of my eyes has to be, by default, the roving eye, always on alert. In heavy seas, it was engaged on quite a different mission than scanning for fish. Here, I had to cast about, ever vigilant to detect the odd rogue wave, those monsters that can be two or three times the size of their companions, vicious waves that could easily add my boat to the long list of vessels that the ocean has entombed.

There would be no possibility of swimming to safety if capsized in such a sea. *Caribeña* was life itself; she must remain afloat.

As I rode the seas, my hands barely had time to firmly turn the wheel. Right, left, right, left, hard right! An occasional

fast left, straightening the course. The pattern repeated itself again and again; I eventually got the knack at guessing
which wave threatened to break on top of my boat. When I
thought I had the right rhythm, a burst of wind and a wild
wave struck *Caribeña* on the starboard bow. I saw ominous
danger looming at me. To avoid being broached in an almost
surely fatal roll, I was forced to execute a brazen two-part
360-degree turn. Wind fought *Caribeña* as I turned her 180 degrees, momentarily putting her in a dangerous following sea.
As soon as she was lifted by the next wave passing underneath her starboard transom, I put the starboard engine on
full throttle, turning the boat completely around until her
bow pointed again into the oncoming waves. Under that
kind of pressure, I realized that, confronted with danger, instinct is faster than reason—and I let instinct prevail. If an
engine had been lost, if the glass had been broken on the
cabin's front windows, if the bilge pumps had been over-
whelmed by the force of overbreaking waves, *Caribeña*'s
safety could have been fatally compromised.

We were moving against the seas and a wind that I later
learned had been clocked at seventy-six miles per hour on
land. The bridge was a whirling veil of sea spray, driven into
my hands and neck. I was transformed into an inverted human pendulum attached to the deck of the flying bridge by
my hinged feet, my hands glued to the wheel. I felt the
strength of the stinging blasts smashing my face.

What can one do in such instances except pray? *Ayudate,*

que te ayudare, as my mother used to say. ("He is helped who helps himself.") Suddenly, I felt a familiar sense of calm. "What will happen is what was meant to be," I thought. Nothing will change that.

Suddenly, I saw first in my radar screen and then ahead, sporadically through the foamy gale and cresting waves, a freighter. Though I had to run the longest three miles of my life, I finally put *Caribeña* side by side on the leeward of that tall, red and yellow ship that it seemed had been sent by the gods. How fast priorities can change at sea with a blowing gale. It didn't matter that I was going south rather than north, as I'd planned. I was now convinced that Norfolk would be a very fine destination, even if it was 100 miles south of my homeport. At least I'd be alive, and *Caribeña* afloat.

Had it not been for the improvised freighter's shield, *Caribeña* probably would have twisted its flying-bridge frames and lost the vinyl enclosures and its bimini top during the storm, the kind of damage that had happened to many other boats close to shore that, unlike *Caribeña*, didn't have a freighter at their side to protect them from the squall.

*

*

*

Many seamen offshore have been concerned seeing *Caribeña* making way, for, as observed from outside, she appears to be an unmanned vessel. But, in reality, through *Caribeña*'s tinted windows, I am constantly on the lookout, maneuvering the automatic pilot's remote control. At the touch of its knob, I have the thirty-two compass's points, eleven and one-quarter degrees for each fourth of a turn, or a whole forty-five degrees in a complete turn of the knob. It's like having a mini-wheel, and I don't have to see the built-in compass all the time to know my course or how many degrees I have to turn to get where I want to go. The Loran-C, with its basic display of time-differential numbers, indicates where I am in the vast ocean. Also of great help when I hook up with a fish is the "memory event" key on the Loran, which registers the exact spot where the fish was raised. That allows me to go back to the same place for another pass. A second VHF radio just twenty inches inside the cabin, with the mike attached to the inside frame of the cabin door, allows me to talk on the radio at the same time I command my boat and fight my prey.

A part of me, the captain's side, loves to ride *Caribeña* for the excitement of the hunt. Reading the waters, anticipating and detecting temperature breaks, seeing currents collide, spotting bait on the run, scanning the surface, or piercing waves trying to see telltale signs of fish among the dark, colorful shadows in the sea—these are the captain's duties. I also love to play mate—keeping an eagle eye on the trolled baits that I've rigged with meticulous attention to detail, watching for marlin to appear behind them, to give the angler the upper hand and prepare himself in advance for the proper drop back.

Well-rigged baits define the mate. Seeing a marlin before

the strike is a big plus. Normally, the mate is also the one with a say in the proper balance of the fishing equipment to be used in each hunt: what kind of bait should be, used and how it will be rigged; the size of the hook, how sharp it should be, and how it's going to be attached to the monofilament leader. The mate decides when to use a reliable Palomar knot or a crimped metal sleeve. The mate chooses the weight or class of the fishing line and checks the reliability of everything—from inspecting the rod and its rollers to the proper lubrication of the mounted reel on its waxed rod seat. It's imperative to calibrate each reel with a smooth drag to sustain a lightning marlin assault. As *Caribeña*'s mate, I decide what kind of leader to use and its length.

As a fish strikes and I become the angler, I store in the mate and captain compartments of my mind why the fish was raised, registering the assortment of baits I was trolling and their spread. What was our course? Up sea? Down sea? Across? Any ripples around? Sea grass? Floating debris? A temperature break? Was there live bait around for the marlin to eat? Which of my baits did the marlin take? Was it skipping? Swimming? Weighted? Naked? Or "sea witched": a lure five or six inches long with nylon fibers that resemble hair with a light weight in its core to keep the bait in the water and help me to see it in a choppy sea? Was there another marlin around? Where was the center rigger bait? How close to the short rigger baits? Everything is important, and every detail counts.

As mate, I have a secret for doubleheaders. Every time a

marlin is on, I put the furthest bait from the fish on free spool for a minute or two. As I control and fight the first fish, I engage the drag of the second reel in free spool, and with the first rod still in the rod holder I *reelreelreelreelreelreel!* as fast as I can with one hand, the boat still going forward at minimum speed, hoping to find the closed mouth of a second marlin around that particular bait and its hook. And sometimes it works! Often there is a second white marlin around, eager to eat. Too often on other boats they make the mistake of reeling in the baits as soon as they have a fish on, killing the chance for a double- (or triple-) header. On *Caribeña*, I have learned to keep the baits in the water until it becomes imperative to retrieve them (to avoid tangling and breaking lines).

I record all strikes on the plotter, or in the Loran, depending on where I am on the boat when the marlin hits, or immediately after, during the first stage of the fight. Once the fight is done and the fish released, we, as captain-mate-and-angler, a team of one, kind of share what we had noticed and go back to the same spot, armed exactly as we were when we made the first successful pass. Same baits, same spread, same speed, and—here it comes (an important trick— a secret!): the same angle of approach. I have learned that more often than not I elicit a second bite at, or very close to, the site marked in the plotter or Loran if I *duplicate the original trolling approach.*

As the angler in my boat, I don't always see what I see

when I am in the role of mate. Called to action, I am more attuned to the coordinating skills, making things happen in the pure and final sense of hooking up and catching the fish. I focus on the fish and the rod, the free spool, the dropping back, being sure that the hook will do its job. I am the last link in the chain formed by the captain's hunt and the skillful preparation of the mate.

Is that all I do on board my *Caribeña*? Not necessarily. I constantly listen to the hum of *Caribeña*'s CATS, often adjusting them to produce the proper pitch. I am engulfed in her mantra that rides through the air. Alone with my thoughts, I feel *Caribeña* gliding, moving us through time. Or is it time that is moving through us? I am mesmerized by her motion and the motion of the sea. But no matter how far away my mind may be, I always return miraculously on time, to hear "the mate" calling out that marlin has risen from the depths.

SEVEN

RIDERS
OF THE STREAM

It took *Caribeña* and me two years to *officially* enter the competitive world of marlin fishing in Ocean City via membership in the local Marlin Club, and it took another two seasons for the inner circle of its 500 members and 150 registered boats to accept us into their tight enclave. I think it was mostly because they didn't know how to react to the unique fact that I fish for marlin alone. They were puzzled, surprised, and highly skeptical of my rumored success.

There had been many sightings of my fighting billfish on *Caribeña* in the deep, and I had brought many a large tuna to the docks; but it wasn't until I participated in a couple of tournaments, which required club observers on board, that this small group had to reckon with a crew of one.

Captain Lee Fickinger came on board *Caribeña* one late

August morning in 1988 at 5:00 A.M. sharp. He had a mission—the club's designated observer assigned to my boat during the White Marlin Light Tackle Tournament, where the angler has to fight his fish from a dead boat (in other words, you can't back the boat toward the fish or move away from the fish if it threatens to go under the boat). In order to earn the 100 points per billfish, one has to release his marlin in less than five minutes. Do it a second after five minutes and the fish is worth only 75 points; after ten minutes, 50 points; after fifteen minutes, only 25 points, and if it takes more than twenty minutes, you earn only 5 points. Without any restrictions, it's tougher than you think to hook, fight, vanquish, and release the fish. To do it in less than five minutes from a dead boat requires a strong mix of dexterity and luck.

The first thing for Lee to do on board *Caribeña* was observe that my fishing would be done according to the rules of the International Game Fish Association. I had to fish twenty-pound test, green Ande Tournament line, and the leader and double line (if any) were not to exceed twenty feet; when the fish struck, the rod had to be promptly removed from the rod holder, and, at any time during the fight, the rod was not allowed to rest on the boat's gunwales and give a respite to the angler. At all times, I had to troll natural dead bait with a single hook. Since I would fish alone, there was no need for Lee to check that someone else on board would help me handle the fish or improperly touch my tackle or line. Break any of these rules and your catch would be disqualified.

If an angler were to fight a marlin, captains would be allowed to keep the engines in neutral only or to simultaneously engage one engine forward and the other on reverse, spinning the boat, in order to present the transom to the fish. But they were not allowed to engage the boat's engines to back down or pursue the fish. If they did so, the catch would also be disqualified. Lee was eager to know how I could possibly manage to keep within these rules and fight fish single-handedly.

Lee, an easygoing guy with a big grin, was a retired undercover cop from Washington, D.C., well known as a competent seaman. He had brought his own stopwatch. Like all the other boats, we went with *Caribeña* to the Norfolk Canyon, eighty miles offshore. Because of the time it took us to cover that distance, we started fishing around the fleet a few minutes after 9:00 (the tournament had officially started at 8:30). The club members on board some thirty private and charter boats had yet to release a billfish, although two or three boats had reported marlin strikes. Ten minutes into my trolling, I was lucky to have a white marlin in pursuit of one of my baits. Under the scrutinizing eyes of Lee, I lifted the rod, dropped back the bait and hooked up the fish, put the engines in neutral, reeled in my two other lines, and proceeded to fight the fish from my dead boat. Exactly four minutes and fifteen seconds from the hook up, I released the fish. A few boats, with their own observers on board, were observing *Caribeña*, and Lee, via the radio microphone on the fly bridge, gave the whole fleet a play-by-play narration of the event.

Hardly had the buzz subsided when *Caribeña* raised a second white marlin. Lift rod, drop back, hook up, neutral, fight, spin with the cockpit controls, fight more, spin again, grab leader, remove hook, and release. All done again from a "dead boat" that proved to be "well tuned and alive." This time, however, according to Lee and his stopwatch, it took me four minutes and forty-five seconds to earn another 100 points. I was glad to have Lee Fickinger on board. Nobody else had caught any fish yet. I couldn't have said what I had done as well as he did, and who knows how many would have doubted my luck.

Over the next few years, several observers came after Lee and confirmed the success of the crew of one. It wasn't until August 1990, when I caught five white marlin in one day, that the ultimate validation of my approach to marlin fishing and my final acceptance into the club came about.

The news of my catches that day spread rapidly throughout the fishing community. The local papers, always in need of a story to write about, picked up on my adventure at Alligator's Bight. Still, there was some skepticism. I knew Ocean City's fishing history. Nobody had ever fished alone far offshore. On average, it would take two, three, four, or even five trips to catch a single billfish. Boats often returned to port day after day without flying a marlin flag. Some of my fellow fisherman would scoff: five white marlin in a day? Alone? Hard to believe! It can't be done, they concluded.

They were from *la vieja guardia*, from the old guard, accustomed to team fishing. And they had also, through most of the 1980s, experienced record-low marlin catches. To make matters worse, one of them—a very good angler by all accounts—was having a particularly difficult time putting a hook into white marlin being raised by his boat. According to the soon-to-be former captain of his boat, this angler had missed, in several trips, a string of twenty-seven marlin strikes. Sometimes it's the angler, sometimes the boat, sometimes the fish. Deep-sea fishing is hit and miss, and nowhere more so than in the deep-sea canyons off Ocean City. The history of the tournaments in this "Marlin Capital of the World" has been shaped by the inconsistency of the catch.

In 1946, four international clubs started a confederation called the International Light Tackle Tournament Association, now known as the ILTTA. An annual competition was organized in which clubs around the world would send teams, each with three anglers, to compete for billfish in different countries, but primarily in Mexico and off both coasts of the United States.

Our own Ocean City Light Tackle Club of Maryland, (OCLTC), was one of the first clubs to join the ILTTA. The club members, accustomed to fishing for white marlin, did not take long to prove their skills. In January 1955, fishing off Palm Beach, they won the tenth ILTTA Tournament as Jim O'Donnell, Allan Ferguson, and Osbourn Owings accumulated 970 points with 14 billfish. In total, 174 billfish were released in three days of fishing, an average of slightly more than two sailfish per boat, per day.

Then, in 1956, the twelfth ILTTA was held in Ocean City, where thirty-three clubs and ninety-nine anglers competed. Only four white marlin were caught and released. Four in one week! No wonder the ILTTA never returned.

For the next thirty years, the fishing was inconsistent. The tallies for the late 1980s were a little better, and the five whites caught in one day in 1989 was good news. In a way, it renewed hope in a fishery that had hit historical lows in 1985 and 1986.

Despite the inconsistency of the marlin fishing, many of the club's boats find solace in another great game fish: the tuna. The tuna, a prodigious fighter in all its different species, perhaps more than any fish, has kept alive the sport-fishing fleets of the mid-Atlantic.

Our fishing season in the mid-Atlantic starts with an early June run of the bluefin tunas. In scientific circles, this species is also identified as Northern bluefin tuna, not to be confused with Southern bluefin tuna found in oceans below the equator. Of all the tunas, bluefin is the one species that comes close to the mid-Atlantic shores, usually running from twenty to thirty miles offshore. They arrive by the hundreds in schools holding fish of similar size and weight, which vary from school to school from 50 to 300-plus pounds.

In their northern migration from Bimini back to the waters of Prince Edward Island, they congregate and feed at the 26 Mile Hill, move on to the Parking Lot, the Lumps, and the Hot Dog, all popular places for chunking and trolling in waters twenty fathoms deep, between 36° N and 38° N latitudes.

The bluefin, one of ten different tunas roaming the oceans of the world, is perhaps the most important species for the gourmet table of the recreational angler who is fishing from his own boat or aboard charter boats. For the charter industry, the bluefin tuna is its bread and butter. Its meat is dark and has tremendous value for the Japanese market of sushi and sashimi. A single fish can be sold on the docks for thousands of dollars, which creates enormous pressure on the species, whose stocks—believed by many to be dwindling—are in desperate need of effective controls.

Although many members of the club go out in early June after tuna, my fishing season doesn't really start until late in the month or early July, despite the fact that every year the Ocean City Marlin Club and the city council of Ocean City open their coffers to offer a combined $6,000 reward for the capture and release of the first white marlin of the season. Offer proof of your catch—a witness or a picture of your fish should be enough—and you will collect the prize. The $6,000 is an incentive to promote the start of the fishing season, which translates into early revenues for the city after its long winter nap.

Since 1937 a white marlin has never been caught before

June eighth. And only three times on that date. I had tried
in the past to catch the first white and do it before the eighth
of June, but I have yet to succeed. More recently, I have
been starting my fishing in July when the chances of a catch
are better, often after the reward has already been claimed.

I start my season once the water temperature jumps over
the seventy-degree mark. I usually hear from other boats
about the first scattered marlin of the year that have shown up
off Ocean City. Generally, white marlin are caught before
blues, perhaps for no other reason than whites seem to toler-
ate water temperatures in the low seventies better than blues,
as well as the fact that this region produces an average of ten
whites for every one blue caught with rod and reel.

Once I start fishing, if friends or charter captains want to
know, I will tell them where I'm catching fish. I'm sure
some guys fishing the canyons out of Ocean City might
think that by doing that I'm from another planet . . . or another country, perhaps. Invariably, I welcome them to try
alongside *Caribeña*. I don't mind sharing with them what
I've been lucky enough to find. This policy has won me
friends at the club and among the charter captains, and they,
in turn, will often share their information with me.

This is important because if there's one thing I've
learned through the years, it is that it's impossible to be at
the right place all the time. Now and then you'll find your-
self lost in a familiar sea, unable to locate the spot where the
strikes and hook ups are taking place. The problem is that

hot spots have never been anchored to the bottom of the sea. Waves don't grow roots. The fish that ignite the spark in our eyes are the gypsies of the open ocean; roaming the seas is the way they live and die. They come and go. They are hard to find.

This is exactly why offshore fishing is so much more difficult and different from all other kinds of fishing. You have to track and hunt over a vast mass of water. If you want to succeed, sometimes you have to be willing to quickly recognize that you've come to the wrong place and move, move like the fish, even if that means picking up baits and running toward the area where there is a bite in progress, which is, hopefully, not far away.

I am very conscious that there is only a fleeting opportunity to line up all the variables involved in a marlin strike. As I lurch for the rod, I simultaneously know what is happening on the spread. I have learned to trust my instincts and my mate's eyes. The tip of the marlin's dorsal fin will dash briefly, slicing the water, disappearing for a second, to reappear defiant and intent.

I know where I am. I know what I have at hand. I point the tip of the rod, like a flashlight, straight at the disappearing line. Feeling the white marlin touching the bait, I let the line go, go, and go some more. Then, with a mixture of reason and instinct, as the fish runs, I pull up the lever on the right curved side of the reel to break the free run of line. A long second elapses before the slack line comes tauten and

I feel the marlin's pull threatening to take the rod from my hands. That's the time to strike back! Done! Fish on! And the fight has just began.

All of us who ride the Gulf Stream feel the same way. Just being there, and hooking up with the mighty white—regardless of the outcome—makes us feel lucky to be alive.

●

●

●

Although I will never be 100 percent sure how much or even if *Caribeña* entices billfish to rise from the depths, I suspect that at least part of our success has to do with the way she prowls through the ripples or swings up and down as she cuts the waves, leaving behind her unique wake, that offshore racetrack for skipping and swimming baits. And there is the other element used to raise fish: the purring of her gutsy cats. But whatever she does . . . it works.

The five marlin in one day in the 1989 season led the club to recognize me in a way that made me feel I was finally one of the guys. That season, *Caribeña* and I were proving ourselves real contenders in the club. We were attempting to prevail in the race to win the honors as the Top Private Boat of the Year in our class. With only one week to fish until the end of the season, *Caribeña* was leading in the category reserved for boats under forty feet, and she was one of the top five boats in the general race. But being more a weekend warrior than a full-time competitor in that general category—usually reserved for the overall deeper pockets—she didn't have a real chance to become number one. The race for that spot was between John Evans's *Magic Marlin* and Bill Fenwick's *Solitaire*, two of the Ocean City Marlin Club's best boats.

Up to that point, the award competition had been neck and neck (or bill and bill) as *Solitaire* and *Magic Marlin* entered the final stretch. *Magic Marlin* decided to bring a lucky angler on board, and John tapped me for the job. I was flattered and readily accepted.

I was expecting to fish with John and his two young sons, John Jr. and Chris, a knowledgeable trio backed by an excellent crew. But when I showed up at the dock, I was greeted by Mark "Hammer" Hill, the captain, and Jimmy Grant, acting as a mate, a pair of young men anyone would like to have on his own boat.

Having arrived a few minutes ahead of the agreed time, I admired the fine carpentry and talented craftsmanship of *Magic Marlin*'s salon. I was surprised when, through the tinted window, I noticed the mate undoing the lines and the captain ready to pull away from the T-dock. There was still no sign of John, John Jr., or Chris.

"What's up, Mark?" I asked.

"We're ready to go," he said from the fly bridge.

"Where's John?" I asked.

"He's not coming!"

"What about the boys?"

"They're starting school today."

"What do you mean?"

"Carlos, I thought you knew!" he said, showing surprise. "You are the team today!" Before I could say anything, he went on: "What's new? You always fish with only one angler on board! Go inside and rest. We'll need you in three hours. It's going to be a hot fishing day."

I had known Mark since his days as a mate and, later, as the captain of *Carter's Ark*, a private fifty-five-foot boat owned by Dick Carter that, in the mid-1980s, had the tragic misfortune of losing its previous captain, Charlie "Tuna" Klemkowsky, to a freak accident when he fell from the top of the boat's tuna tower while docked at Cape May.

Mark had taken over as captain of *Carter's Ark*, and we had often talked on the radio while fishing offshore. I had fished one time on *Carter's Ark*, where fifty-pound test line was the lightest tackle on board, and I had invited Mark to fish on *Caribeña* in turn, so he could see for himself the advantages and the sporty side of fishing for marlin with light tackle using twenty-pound test. Mark was knowledgeable about the intricacies of offshore fishing but new to light tackle, and, like Bob Lord before him (the first captain of *The Elixir*), he caught his first white marlin on twenty-pound line aboard *Caribeña*. Those two professional captains were thrilled and quickly converted to light-tackle fishing.

Mark revved up *Magic Marlin* to thirty-plus knots once we were outside the Ocean City inlet. He had done his homework and knew where the bite had been the day before; he knew the ins and outs of the area we were on our way to troll. He was acutely aware that *Solitaire*, with thirty-four white marlin caught and leading by four whites, wouldn't be fishing that September day, which meant that all the marlin in the Atlantic were *Magic Marlin*'s for the taking.

The forecast for the day was overcast skies, some rain, winds from the north, blowing in the upper teens, with expected gusts of twenty to twenty-five mph offshore. But we didn't care. Personally, I felt as if I were on a crusade.

By early afternoon, working with a captain and mate, I had been able to concentrate only on *catching* the fish and had hooked up, fought, and released four white marlin. By virtue of two doubleheaders, we had a total of six billfish to add on to *Magic Marlin*'s column of billfish released.

Mark's prediction about a hot fishing day had been on target, I thought, as we returned to shore in the middle of the storm. High winds and tricky seas showcased the big difference between a large fifty-foot-plus boat and *Caribeña*'s thirty-five feet. However, the sense of accomplishment flying those flapping marlin flags was almost the same.

As we turned north on the back bay and went through the lifted Route 50 bridge, another squall unleashed its fury. Mark, sensing the danger of being caught in the narrow passage that leads up to the slip, had to hold his boat on the bay for fifteen minutes or more, bow to the winds, before coming into the basin of Harbour Island to dock. John Evans's clan was waiting at the dock with big smiles.

Although the bad weather persisted for a few days, a

small window of fair seas and moderate winds allowed *Solitaire* to regain the lead and prevail in the end. *Solitaire* would be the Top Private Boat of the Year closely followed by *Magic Marlin*.

Up to this point, *Caribeña* had been leading in the Most Billfish Caught in One Day category from my five white marlin, but by catching the six billfish with *Magic Marlin*, I had defeated myself. I didn't pay any attention to this, genuinely happy about the success I'd had, and satisfied that I had helped the Evanses in their quest. However, somebody, somehow, had noticed how the events unfolded. And while they gave the Most Billfish Caught in One Day Award to *Magic Marlin* that year, the club created the Outstanding Sportsmanship Award and bestowed it on *Caribeña* and her crew of one. I felt like one of the boys, fully accepted into the fraternity.

.

.

.

After my day on *Magic Marlin*, I thought I would go out once more that season. But soon the winds blew up out of the northeast, the water temperature dropped, and the marlin headed down the Gulf Stream to warmer climes.

I woke to the wind one morning and decided to go look at the sea. The beach was unseasonably empty. All was water and sky as far as I could see. Not a single person was out, not a single swimmer, or boat. No commercial ships had left the inlet, and no one had come in from the sea, seeking refuge in the calm waters of the back bay.

The winds blew hard, and the ocean, in spite of being agitated and murky, still looked immensely attractive, almost seductive, inviting me for a dangerous rendezvous, which I prudently declined. Instead, I went back to *Caribeña* and spent hours fixing, mending, tightening, and replacing what in previous offshore trips had been broken, loosened, and bent.

There had been times when the prevailing and deceptive west winds of early fall made it easy for *Caribeña* to reach the fishing grounds. But when it was time to return to port, heading into the seas, the punishment *Caribeña* and I took was a kind of hell. I would have to start back at noon if I wanted to dock by 7:00 P.M. The boat seemed to crawl; its cruising speed seven knots. On those occasions, I've been lucky and have not lost the boat or had her windows smashed. But her screws have loosened, and each of my muscles and nerves has felt the strain of those journeys. And the punishment the west winds have inflicted on me and *Caribeña* has been mild when compared with those unleashed by the northeast gales that often buffet Ocean City.

Noon that day found me seated at a table in the Captain's Galley with a friend, having a hot meal—for a change—and a tall glass of iced tea, relaxed, chatting about, what else, fishing offshore. From the restaurant window, I saw all the boats tied at the dock. Nobody had gone out to fish. After lunch, I went back to *Caribeña* and rearranged rigged baits and added salt to them.

Except for two large split-tail mullets with eight-ounce egg sinkers secured under their chins, the baits were small ballyhoo I planned to use for my last expedition of the year. I reset the drags on the reels, checked lines for abrasions and debilitating nicks, made new leaders, and, using my finest file—the small one kept clean with white vinegar and a dental brush—I resharpened the already sharp hooks. A very sharp hook can give the angler the cutting edge needed to produce a release from an otherwise missed fish.

I estimate that for every thirty-five or so marlin I've caught, one has been foul hooked. That occurs when I miss the initial strike, and the fish, on the run, is caught by that extra-sharp point of the hook that allows it to penetrate the thin, small scales protecting the fish's skin. Usually the area of the snag tends to be behind the marlin's head, on the black side between the upper part of the gill plate and the base of the tallest part of the dorsal fin. A few times the fish has been hooked up between the anal fin and the base of the forked tail, on the caudal fins—the area that I would call its "ankles" if I were to apply human anatomy to marlin. A foul-hooked marlin is hard to fight and can be dangerous by the boat if still "green," or uncooperative and wild.

If a marlin, with its propensity to jump, acts borderline shy, sounds, and is reluctant to come up, I immediately suspect a foul-hooked fish, and the first thing I do is to ease

even more my normally light drag. Depending on how far
or deep the fish is, even a four- or five-pound drag can be too
much to successfully bring the fish to the boat and have a
release. Inadequate patience, excessive drag, or a bad combination with too little of the first and too much of the other
can result in a pulled hook or even a broken line. Patience
is key. A normal five-minute fight can be prolonged to
twenty, twenty-five, or thirty minutes if the hook is not in
the marlin's mouth. If you want the fish, you have to wait.

Although I had planned to, I didn't travel again that season
out to the deep canyons. The winds kept up, and it turned
out that the only challenge I faced was to be on time for
restaurant reservations. In one of the restaurants was a new
chef, with a novel approach, and, to my delight, he proved to
have an authoritative culinary hand. The relative balance
between the flavors of the ingredients was as perfect as it
gets. Cooking, I think, is like writing, or rigging baits. Success depends on talent and on fine details. There are those
blessed with the art, skill, or craft to create *una obra de arte* in
each thing they prepare, attracting epicurean mouths, sensi-
tive minds, or predatory, hungry fish, as the billed beasts of
the seas.

But even those who possess talent and skills can find success fleeting. I knew this when my restaurants were running
at their peak. I knew that even well-rehearsed schemes
could change in a moment. Sportfishing is as deeply satisfy-

ing to me as running restaurants, and even though I'm considered successful at both, I don't depend on success to enjoy the action at sea. I also know that tragedy could strike at any time.

This happened to Captain Chris Bowie, who was only twenty-nine years old when he died. His story needs to be kept alive to remind all of us that venturing to sea to fish for marlin is a dangerous, even deadly, game.

A thin line separates life from death. Often a human life hangs by a thread. But, in Chris's case, on June 16, 1994, it was just the reverse: a line, in this case a thin wire that did not break, cost him his life.

I have kept the sketchy press accounts of his death in a bottom drawer of *Caribeña*'s v-berth, knowing that there would be a time that I'd want to examine the circumstances surrounding this freak event. Up and down the coasts of North and Central America, Chris was known in the fishing circles as a competent man of the sea. I had known him for years as a mate on boats of his mentor, Capt. Joe Riley, and later as captain of an Ocean City boat called *Midnight Hour*. Our paths had crossed at the Harbour Island's docks, and we had fished the same offshore grounds.

In June 1994, Chris's fishing skills and reputation had earned him an invitation to fish with Captain Alan Fields aboard the *Trophy Box*, a private fifty-three-foot Carolina-built boat. Chris would be part of an experienced team, for the whole crew had been exposed to the offshore game.

Chris joined mates Jimmy and Ronnie Fields, Alan's sons, to participate in the Big Rock Blue Marlin Tournament out of Morehead City, North Carolina. *Trophy Box* and 165 other boats would compete for a $500,000 purse.

Two days of the tournament had been uneventful, but on the third day of fishing, an under-200-pound blue marlin struck one of the trolled baits. The fish was promptly hooked up, but the hook hadn't lodged in its mouth, but on top of its head.

Connected to a foul-hooked fish, it took forty-five minutes for one of the anglers on board to reel in the blue close to the boat, and, being foul hooked, the blue was still "green": full of energy, wild. Nevertheless, Chris, an expert wireman, properly wrapped the wire leader around the palm of his gloved hands, one loop at a time. One wrap and pull, and then, with the other hand, a wrap and pull while undoing the previous wrap and freeing the other hand to start all over again. Take more than two wraps and the pressure of the fish pulling away can tighten the wraps and lock them around the wireman's hand. And, if the wraps lock, the wireman can become permanently fastened to the wild beast, which is just what happened to Chris.

I have been aboard the *Trophy Box* several times. I know its cockpit, the stage where the fatal accident occurred. I have fished with the Fields, and they would be at the top of my best teams list. There was no indication that anyone aboard that boat, including Chris, had done anything wrong.

Wrap after wrap and the marlin was on the port side of the boat. It was too small to be boated. Jimmy Fields tagged the fish.

But then, the instant the marlin felt the tag, it went berserk. It surged in a desperate jump toward the front of the boat, half of its black body and its menacing bill out of the water. Chris—still wired to the fish—was braced with his legs against the port bulkhead of the *Trophy Box*. The wire came tense, and the fish at its end abruptly turned 180 degrees, and, again, parallel to the hull, port to port, its bill now pointing toward the wake left by the boat, catapulted away at full speed.

Chris faced out from the port side of the boat. He turned to his left, his right hand wrapped around the wire, his right arm lifted and extended, pointing to the blue in the boat's wake, but his legs, still three feet from the transom wall, were without support; it was as if he were being pulled on a leash by a running dog. Before his legs reached the bulkhead, he was yanked overboard.

Chris, visible three feet below the surface of the water, was trying to unwrap his hand from the wire while slowly being pulled by the marlin. To compound the situation, the fishing line behind Chris, which had been connected to the wire leader, broke.

Ronnie Fields climbed to the top of the transom, pliers in hand, ready to jump overboard when Alan, his father, from the flying bridge told him not to. It's possible that if

Ronnie had gone into the water with the intention of bringing Chris to the surface or cutting the wire to set him free, the splash from his diving would have spooked the marlin, igniting a faster run to the depths.

Sadly, the blue dived anyway, hauling Chris to his death. Jimmy could do nothing to help his friend. Owner, anglers, and guests on board were horrified. Captain Fields could only observe in despair.

The message was clear. Even when everything seems to be done properly, tragedy can strike. Many times, as the wire tightens around my own hand, as I bring a marlin alongside *Caribeña*, I remember Chris. Wrap, let go, wrap, let go. He taught us all a powerful lesson: we must never take for granted the power contained in these beautiful, wild, and potentially deadly creatures that we hunt.

EIGHT

•

•

PRINCE
OF THE OCEAN

TUESDAY, AUGUST 6, 1996

When I went to bed the night before, I didn't expect to go
fishing the next day, planning instead to declare the first of
the two non-fishing days I am allowed in the week. I
thought I would need rest and figured I would probably
sleep until 8:00 A.M., have breakfast, spend the day preparing bait, and wait to see what kind of fish and how many
were caught and released by the boats that had decided to
go out. But the day didn't turn out as planned.

It was 4:45 A.M. when I was awakened by the combined
thundering of who-knows-how-many engines igniting almost
simultaneously. The marina was suddenly a frantic place, almost febrile, as boat after boat shuddered out of its berth

and into the narrow channel, all on their way to the deep, to bring home the glory and gold.

I was perforce awake. Standing at the dock, I said good-bye and wished luck to so many boats that soon it looked as if *Caribeña* and I were the only ones left in town. The marina was empty. And I *felt* empty, orphaned. I knew then and there that I had to go fishing; otherwise, what would I do with the rest of such a long day? A day that, like the one before, had opened to a beautiful morning, very calm, with no wind, just a breeze, and no clouds.

It didn't take me long to change my plans. I jumped into *Caribeña*, put two cinnamon-raisin bagels into the electric oven and three twelve-packs of frozen medium-sized bally-hoo on the fish box—to be rigged under way. I added some oil to the engine before I turned on the CATS and started the electronics. Then I jumped down from the bridge and undid *Caribeña*'s five mooring lines. Typically the first to leave, we were that day the last to depart. In fact, by the time she was under way, there was enough daylight so that she didn't need running lights.

We went quickly under the open drawbridge, through the inlet, beyond the sea buoy, all the way to the five-mile red buoy. Behind *Caribeña*, I saw a clutch of small boats, but none up ahead was silhouetted against the eastern horizon—a re-minder of how late I was for my second day of fishing.

It was another day of unusual calm. I decided to go north, close to the tip of Baltimore Canyon, even though I knew that a seventy-three-pound white marlin had been caught inside Washington Canyon—and was so far the tournament's leading fish. Checking the chart and the Loran, entering the numbers of my intended destination on the grid, I calculated that it would take me about two hours and forty-five minutes to arrive at the edge and start fishing. It meant I would be putting the lines in the water at 9:15, forty-five minutes after the official starting time.

I felt disappointed when I saw the small floaters that mark submerged traps for whelk—a local variation of conch— for I knew they were only five or six miles offshore. The radar showed nothing for three, six, twelve miles ahead. Ten miles later, I saw another kind of floating marker, dozens and dozens of poles with small triangular white flags that signal sea bass grounds between sixteen and twenty-two miles from the coast. They float in lineal pairs 1,800 feet apart. One pole is anchored to a rectangular wooden or wire trap, set close to natural structures or wrecks on the ocean floor, 80 or 100 feet below, where sea bass are likely to find clams, crabs, and worms to eat. The second floating pole is attached to the last of a set of fifteen traps, all connected by line. No bait is involved for this catch. Sea bass come into the trap instinctively looking for protection. In the late 1990s, a licensed commercial fisherman was allowed to keep as much as 1,500 pounds of bass each day.

I felt my spirits lift when I passed a group of commercial draggers working in tandem around the twenty-five- to thirty-fathom lines. With them astern, I periodically checked the radar, and the horizon, too, keeping an eye out for the occasional commercial ship, the only kind of vessel I expected to find, until reaching the fifty-fathom line, which was one hour away. If I didn't see something interesting floating on the water, like seaweed, or detect a temperature break, to alter my plans, I would run another twenty nautical miles before I cut my speed and started to troll.

In spite of having some rigged bait from the previous day, in an acute attack of optimism I rigged twelve more ballyhoos for white marlin and also two horse ballyhoos—preceded by a resplendent white-and-blue Hawaiian-eye lure—a favorite blue marlin snack.

In addition to a seventy-three-pound white marlin caught by John Brown, Jr. on the *Outer Limits* from Pirate's Cove, North Carolina, Monday's catch included a blue marlin, boated by someone I didn't know. It weighed in at 308 pounds. Those were the fish I had to beat.

It was 9:15 when I arrived at the tip of the Baltimore Canyon. I looked around and I didn't like what I saw: not only green water, instead of blue, but seventy-three degrees—in lieu of the expected seventy-six. Two radio calls and two minutes later, I learned that the boats I saw scattered around me had been trolling since 8:30 without any luck. I slowed down to fifteen knots, trying to find something, anything, to use as a decent starting point.

9:30 A.M.: Although things were improving—the water had an accent of blue and was seventy-four—I felt the pressure mounting with the ticking of the clock. It was understandable to presume that I would have a better chance of catching fish if I put my baits in the water—any water—than if they were chilling in the cooler. Since it was clear from what I heard on the radio that there had not been much action, I was calm. I stopped *Caribeña* and trolled four medium ballyhoos from the outriggers. From the shotgun center rigger, I pulled a horse ballyhoo to entice a big blue. It was still very calm. Maybe too calm for billfish to strike.

11:30 A.M.: Nothing on the baits. With the flat sea, I'd upped my normal trolling speed of 5.2 knots to 5.8, which, watching the action of the baits, still seemed slow. I raised my speed a half-knot to 6.3, and the baits perked up and started to swim with a taunting gait on *Caribeña*'s slightly wider and foamier wake.

1:30 P.M.: With not much else to do than watch the baits enjoying their bite-less ride, I started eating my lunch, hoping for a marlin to interrupt my meal.

2:30 P.M.: Nothing yet. I changed and moved the baits several times, longer and shorter, in and out, but obviously no pelagic noticed, or cared.

3:15 P.M.: Not a single touch the whole day. I changed the short rigger baits one more time, stationed myself next to the cockpit controls, and played what I thought of as my last-minute game plan. I periodically disengaged the engines, slowing *Caribeña* to a three-knot speed, then reengaged them, a stop-and-start procedure that I hoped would give new life to my sluggishly swimming bait.

3:24 on my wristwatch—3:20, I am sure, on the committee boat, meaning ten more official minutes of fishing to go. The baits were sinking again, and the message from my eyes to my heart almost made the latter explode: white marlin on the short port rigger! I picked up my rod before the fish picked up the bait. The order was essential. It gave me the advantage of being poised for the fight, while the fish, sensing no tension on the line, was not wary enough to reject the bait. I dropped back in free spool, and just after the marlin disappeared, I saw it on the other side of the boat, behind the daisy chain of squids.

It was such a fast fish to dart down and surge up with renewed impetuosity on the other side of the boat! But a second later, I realized that was not what had happened at all. I was losing line fast from the reel in my hands; the fish was running with my bait. Therefore it could not be behind the teaser. A *second* white marlin was hitting the squid!

Typical for marlin fishing. Nothing for hours and hours—absolutely *nada*—and then, suddenly, almost too much at the same time for any crew, but particularly for a crew of one.

I engaged the drag, and my rod bent as the line abruptly slowed down and for an instant stopped. I struck, lifting the rod—two, three times. The marlin was on, hooked up, jumping and jumping on my port side. Meanwhile, the second white had moved away from the teaser; it was now behind the starboard bait, unaware of, or indifferent to, what had just befallen its brother.

I jumped to the starboard side rod and grabbed it with my right hand. Just as the second marlin charged to take the bait, I opened the drag full, putting the reel in free spool. The boat was still moving forward. While the first fish sounded, I switched hands: the hooked-up rod now went in my right hand while my left took hold of the second rod's reel. I lifted the rod, feeling the line speed through my ring and middle fingers, and set the butt end of the rod in the rod belt to support the upcoming strike. As I lowered the rod's tip, I moved the reel's drag up with my thumb. With just one hand, I couldn't reel in to take the slack out of the line, but the boat's forward motion took care of that. The line tensed, and when the marlin on the run tried to take the rod out of my hand, I struck just once, hard, causing the line to sing its crescendo fugue, the most beautiful song you can hear when fishing offshore.

I had my hands full. Literally. A doubleheader just minutes before the mandatory quitting time. *Un regalo del cielo.* A gift from the gods of the sea.

The first fish, having dived deep, still took line, though with less drag, and the second now surfaced, taking its anger out on the leader, but not for long. It, too, sounded, though on the starboard side. There was no chance that the lines would cross.

I stashed my second rod on the starboard side, put the boat in neutral, and started to reel in the first marlin. As soon as the line became tight again, I reeled in the teaser connected to the transom rod.

I heard a couple of boats announce that they'd hooked fish, and I did the same, quickly grabbing the radio microphone from just inside the salon door. "Committee boat, committee boat: Boat two thirty-seven hooked up," I said, panting. "It's a doubleheader."

"Carlos," a voice answered, but he didn't insist on conversation. Perhaps he realized that there was no way I could talk.

Quickly, I had the first fish alongside. The black dacron line wound onto the reel. It was an official release. I tagged the fish swiftly and then, with no time to grab a glove, I took the bill of the fish with my bare hand and twisted out the hook.

One down. One to go.

Since time counted in case of a tie, I wanted to announce my tag and release, but I was anxious to start reeling in my second marlin. I lifted my second rod, hoping the fish was still at the end of the line.

I reeled in the slack, fast, but was unable to tighten the line, so I engaged the engines and put on some speed. It seemed to me that the second fish was gone. But then the rod bent again. I was very glad to be wrong.

Backing with one engine at a time, I soon found myself with an almost vertical fishing line descending straight down some 300 feet. The fish was acting funny—and heavy, although I had thought it was a rather small marlin when it attacked the teaser.

Foul hooked? Have I hooked this fish somewhere other than its mouth?, I wondered. Perhaps. But I couldn't be sure. I put some distance between the line and the transom as I moved the boat forward again. The angle formed by horizontal rod and vertical line increased to 120 or more. Now seemed a good moment to announce my first marlin.

"Committee boat: Boat two thirty-seven. Tagged and released a white marlin two minutes ago. I am still fighting the second one."

"Three thirty-three," responded the committee boat, referring to the time. Then someone added, "Good job! Call us back with the second release."

It took a little time. The marlin, though it was no heavier than forty-five pounds, was tail-wrapped. I tagged him with no resistance, then filmed him with my camcorder. He offered no complaint when I removed the hook from his mouth, so I tried to revive him while holding his bill and keeping him moving forward in the water with the forward motion of the boat. He was pale and obviously weak, but he finally kicked his tail, rolled his big black eyes as if noticing the boat for the first time, then seemed to wave a thank-you with his dorsal fin before swimming slowly to the depths.

"Committee boat."

"Go ahead."

"Tagged and released a white marlin."

"Three forty-two. Great job, Carlos. Great job."

What a day it had been. Starting out as a time of intended rest and in-port observation, it proceeded through several fruitless hours of trolling to that split second when everything changed because two marlin showed up virtually at the same time. I came back into port flying two inverted white marlin flags, posting 150 more points for *Caribeña* and me. In two days of slow fishing, I was three for three. I couldn't complain.

WEDNESDAY, AUGUST 7, 1996

This was it. My third and last day in the twenty-third WMOT. A couple of blue marlin had been caught yesterday, one weighing 446 pounds, but no more white marlin had been added to the board. John Brown's 73.5 pounder was still in the lead in the money category. If nobody else caught a bigger white marlin, Brown and the *Outer Limits* bunch could win more than $400,000, believed to be a world record for a single fish.

Caribeña was the leading boat in the Released Billfish category, and so far, at 225 points for my three tagged and released white marlin, I was the leading overall angler. But I wondered about my odds of winning the tournament. After all, there were still another 236 boats with full crews pursuing the same goal, and there were still three days in which they could fish. I could perhaps as easily re-catch the same three marlin I had just released into the immensity of the Atlantic Ocean as come away the winner against this field.

It was likely that the two previous days had fished out the close-in fishing grounds, so on this day, I decided to move to new turf to do my hunting. I would go to the Washington Canyon and fish the 800-800 square, a popular spot two miles square that takes its name from the intersection of Loran-C time differential lines. The 800-800 is almost on the edge of the 100-fathom line—that is, 600 feet deep. My "Plan B" was to try the even deeper waters around and above the 471- and 500-fathom "Lumps," two submerged hills whose plateaus are 2,800 and 3,000 feet deep, three miles apart, located some five miles outside of the northeast wall of the Washington Canyon.

It was a three-hour ride to the 800-800, but between singing, thinking, and rigging baits, time went by quickly. It was yet another morning of unbelievably flat seas and clear skies. In almost twenty years of fishing the mid-Atlantic, I couldn't remember such wonderful conditions for such an extended time in a month like August, known along the coast as being temperamental and storm prone. It seemed like the the water had been ironed overnight. Not a ripple was to be found in this enchanted calm.

But the weather break beneficial to boats and men did not help the fishing, which had been very poor overall. In two days of trolling, the whole tournament fleet had caught only fifty white marlin and three blue marlin. That worked out to only one fish for every eight boat days.

Unlike yesterday, today I was on time—ready to go at 8:15 A.M., ready to find out what kind of fishing day this would be. "Eight twenty-five," the starter's voice rang out. Five minutes to starting time! Once more, I checked that the swivel's snaps at the end of each line were perfectly closed, ensuring a smooth transition from line to leader. I made sure that rods and butts were firmly connected. For the third time, I confirmed the tension of the drags, even though I knew it was right. All this is the offshore way of killing time, the equivalent, I guess, of the ritual of swinging bats before stepping to the plate in baseball.

Two minutes to starting time. I climbed the ladder for one last trip up to the bridge. I checked every gauge, then looked once more at the radar screen. There were so many boats around! Fifty or sixty, maybe even more in a radius of three miles. I set the course for *Caribeña* away from the fleet at trolling speed.

"Eight thirty," the starter called. "Lines in the water. Good luck!"

"That's what I need," I said aloud.

Demonstrating uncharacteristic restraint, I started the day with only four baits. Of course, I was also dragging my perennial daisy chain of six dancing rubber squid, one of which had been retired to the lead position from the last position after a vicious marlin attack. It was barely held in one piece by careful stitching; the next two squids in line were showing cuts and mutilations—proof of having done a good job enticing predators.

Despite the wear and tear, the whole sextet seemed to be working fine—but what, after all, attracts marlin? Are they lured by dancing squid or by the shape or color of a boat's hull? By the sound of boat engines as they make headway? By what boats drag in their wake as seen from the fish-eye view, when the billfish is looking up? Are marlin attracted to movement of the swift troll? What about voices from the cockpit? Do they like music to be played on board? If so, classical or country?

There was always more to experiment with, more to explore—based on experience, something I'd read, or a hunch. For example, throughout this tournament I had been fishing two large baits during the early morning hours up to about 10:30 A.M., hoping for a matutinal blue marlin strike. If it showed up and I hooked it, I would have time to fight a large fish for several hours, without thinking too much about the clock eating time. An early strike would give me a better chance to fight, gaff, and boat a large fish and get back to the dock on time, before the deadline of fifteen minutes after midnight.

Just like the previous day, the hours were coming and going without a single strike. Now and then, at rare long intervals, somebody would call the committee boat to announce a release. The radio was crackling, however, with captains complaining how slow the fishing had been.

It was afternoon: time for Plan B. I headed out deeper,

reaching for the 500-fathom hills—3,000 feet deep—of the offshore Lumps.

12:45 P.M.: I was close to the southern submerged hill of the Lumps, already being fished by five boats crisscrossing the area. *Miss Allied* was one of them. I could see from far away the pink hue of her hull side and the tall, beautiful silhouette as she moved like a feline huntress against the background of the misty-blue, cloudless sky. David Sherman and his wife, Terry, were in the cockpit. Glenn Mumford was their captain, a man of vast experience. Glenn knew everything there was to know about deep-sea fishing in this region; he'd provide *Miss Allied*'s anglers the best opportunities, so all they would have to do was fight fish that he located.

All the boats were trolling counterclockwise. I was adjusting my angle of entrance into this fishing carousel when the sea surface temperature alarm called insistently from *Caribeña*'s bridge. So that was why these boats were fishing this side of the Lump: there was a temperature break. Weeds marked the edge of a current. For the first time in several days, I felt a sustained breeze and saw a ripple where the weed-marked current converged with another. I had finally found what I'd been looking for since 8:30 A.M. This was a good spot and a good time. For some reason, in general, I tend to be a better, or perhaps a luckier, fisherman later in the day. In this imperfect circle of trolling boats, *Caribeña* was at 6:00.

"*Miss Allied . . . Caribeña*. Are you in this one, Glenn?"

"Go ahead, Carlos."

"Glenn, what's going on here?"

"Not much. There's a break. I marked bait on the depth finder. So far, the fleet has two or three fish up, one released. What did you see?"

"Nothing yet. There were a few marlin released around the tip of Washington Canyon, but not many. And those catches were early in the day." I paused. "I like this area," I added.

"Well, we're trying," said Glenn. "Good luck to you."

"Thanks. The same. We'll talk."

Because they tended to troll faster than most in the Ocean City fleet, boats from Cape May, New Jersey, were easy to recognize. Now one of these "Jersey boats" crossed some 200 yards in front of my bow; he was trolling at eight or nine knots and showing me his port side, just starting to turn into a southerly arc. I had to slow down a notch and turn slightly toward my starboard side to avoid his long center rigger bait trolled far behind his boat; its large lure darted just a few yards in front of *Caribeña*. It was a birdlike, plumed, darting lure, trailed by a Hawaiian eye lure with a horse ballyhoo. The whole assemblage seemed to be proving a very effective bait, receiving abundant attention from many anglers and lots of strikes from the fish.

The Jersey boat and I kept a parallel opposite course, port to port, while I fished the cold side of the break. I wanted to see the name on the boat, but—pop!—the wonderful sound of monofilament being yanked from its holding pin alerted me to the line descending from the short outrigger on my port side. Finally, I had a strike!

I picked up my rod, but nothing tugged at the bait. I could see it skipping on *Caribeña*'s own wake, just a few feet beyond where it had been when the line was first yanked. Had I snagged some grass, perhaps? I didn't know. I didn't think so—there didn't seem to be any on the bait or any loose pieces around.

Could it be a peanut dolphin—a small, maybe two- to three-pound mahimahi? *Tal vez!*—Perhaps! I waited with the rod in my left hand, lifting my arm. The drag was off the reel, but I kept my thumb on the line. Despite lifting the rod as high as I could, my hopes were sinking fast: it was fifteen maybe twenty seconds after the strike, and still nothing had popped up behind the ballyhoo.

I kept my eyes glued to the bait and used peripheral vision to check the baits on *Caribeña*'s starboard side and on her long port rigger, confident that, in such calm seas, if something popped up, I would notice it immediately. Half a minute went by . . . a minute, and still not a single sign of life. I needed to find out, if I had a bite, that the bait was still right. I reeled in and checked the ballyhoo. Nothing was wrong with it. There were no marks on its flesh, nor was the leader chafed.

I was convinced that no marlin had knocked down the line from the clip. Perhaps a mahimahi passed by it but missed the bait, or maybe it had just been some sargasso seaweed. I reloaded the line on the unlocked pin of the outrigger halyard and checked the automatic-pilot remote control to see where I had been heading when whatever it was had happened—it showed 110 degrees. I turned *Caribeña* 180 degrees to retrace our course.

Trolling along the edge of the current marked by sargasso grass, as I reached the spot, it was pretty clear I was the only one showing up. No fish was there to dignify my bait. I still liked the area, though, and I also noticed that there had been two or three calls to the committee boat in the last ten minutes. I looked very closely again at the baits, especially the short rigger baits and in particular at *Caribeña*'s starboard short rigger bait, slightly behind the teaser. It seemed to be *Caribeña*'s hotter spot. But it was cool during this pass over the site.

I turned *Caribeña* around again and yet again. The other boats had noticed my ups and downs over the same spot; they headed closer, perhaps inferring that I had raised something to justify my persistence. One of the boats was charging from my port side, less than half a mile away. It was the Jersey boat again. It trolled easily on this placid sea at a speedy nine or ten knots. Another boat was coming up on my starboard side and would pass me soon. *Miss Allied* was out of the picture. The last time I had seen her, she was some two miles up north.

In my mind, a strike is always just a second away. Now I

was feeling a more insistent premonition. So I was at a high pitch of readiness when a white marlin, advancing like a torpedo in the calm waters, showed up for its afternoon meal. Starboard side. Short rigger. The hotter spot, as advertised. The marlin had ignored *Caribeña*'s daisy chain and gone straight for the ballyhoo. I free spooled to the marlin, letting him run. Pop! There was a yank on the short rigger on the port side. Evidently, starboard wasn't the only hot spot: here was another strike.

After five full hours of *nada*, I suddenly had what was virtually a phantasmagoria—two white marlin appearing as if by magic behind both short rigger baits. I felt two pulses pounding hard: one in my chest, the other in the middle of my head. I knew this feeling well. It was the excitement of the game, this unpredictable game of offshore fishing. I had placed my bet, and I was hoping for two winning cards. The first fish was quick to grab the bait and run. Now with equal speed I gave a short drop back and closed the drag. With no slack in my twenty-pound line, I felt a pull and struck assertively to drive the hook into the marlin's mouth and the whole fish into the air.

Both the marlin and my joy disappeared within seconds— the fish was swallowed by the sea after its convoluted leaps, and my happiness absorbed by the worry that I hadn't had time to react to the second marlin, whose bill had simply nudged the second bait but had not yet grasped it in his jaws.

Because I didn't want to lose an already hooked-up,

semi-caught marlin in order to have a chance at catching a not-yet-hooked, uncaught marlin, I held tight with my right hand to the active rod cupped snugly in my rod belt. With *Caribeña*'s engines engaged and the vessel still moving forward, the line stayed taut as the hooked fish fought for its freedom. Now, with my left hand, I grabbed for the rod on the port side. Leaving the rod inserted in its holder, I released the drag lever of the reel—ready to let the line flow free—but rested my thumb lightly on the line. Just at that moment, the white marlin took the bait in its mouth and angled away from *Caribeña*, clutching what he no doubt assumed was a free lunch.

I let the line run. The fish's excitement was showing in its electric-blue color—its bill and back were virtually neon bright. A click in the reel sounded the alarm, and my naked thumb just barely felt the hot friction of peeling line. The clicking noise intensified. I waited, but not too long, then closed the drag. For a long moment, I felt an anxious knot between the lower ribs in my chest as I waited for the test line to come tight. I struck; the rod bent, recoiled, and bent again, as if bowing to the strength of the marlin now slowed by the stretched and singing line. I saw the white fifty yards away as it extended its pectoral fins like wings and flew on the air. Then it seemed to be walking over the ocean, its forked tail skimming the surface like legs.

I reduced *Caribeña*'s speed, then reeled in both reels, one at a time, still holding one rod in my left hand and reaching for the other one in the starboard holder. If I was not gaining on the two fish, I was at least controlling the lines.

An approaching boat on my starboard side must have seen my frenetic cockpit dance on the deck of *Caribeña*. The captain turned the boat, showed me its stern, and gave me the necessary room to concentrate on my double fight. Three hundred yards later, the boat turned around and came back, trolling at a prudent distance as if looking for a third fish.

I felt the joy coming back; there was a smile on my face as I fought my second doubleheader in two days. Slow as the fishing had been, I found it hard to believe my luck. Pumping and reeling with all the speed and energy I could muster, I put pressure on the first fish, the starboard fish. I sensed him tiring and let him feel that I was not, although I certainly felt the urge to finish this as soon as I could. The portside rod, meanwhile, was still on hold. I paused to reel in its line. *Caribeña* was drifting, but both lines lacked slack. If I'd plucked either one, it would have sounded a high musical note.

The challenge was to bring in the starboard marlin without running over the port line *or* over the other two lines still in the long riggers. I needed to show the fish who was boss by turning its head around so I could bring it to the boat. I finally succeeded, pulling in the black dacron line that I use as a trace in my twenty-foot leader. As it touched the tip of the rod, I scored an official release—seventy points.

I grabbed the leader with my right hand and inserted my rod in the rod holder, then wrapped the line around my hand to bring the fish up to the boat. Quickly, I reached for the tagging pole on the teak cover of the fishing box. Thinking of that second marlin at the end of an increasingly limp line, I knew I had to hurry: I didn't want to lose the second fish for five tagging points. To bring the fish within tagging range required pressure on the leader, but suddenly, in a violent jerk followed by a wild jump to freedom, the leader wrapped in my hand broke at the crimp. Officially released, the fish went off, free, untagged, and with my hook still in the corner of its mouth.

I was bothered by that. The lack of a tag cost me five points and the opportunity to remove the hook. I had been so close. But I couldn't dwell on it. I had tried and done my best. Anyway, there was no time to experience regret for five possible points. There wasn't even time to announce my release to the committee boat or to feel good about the seventy points earned. There was still the second fish. I engaged *Caribeña*'s engines in a forward motion again and quickly lifted my second rod. I reeled in and in and in—but where was the second fish?

I saw the line piercing the water, slicing toward the right. Then, what a relief, the line came tight. The tip of the rod bent and immediately curved into an arc. The fish had swum deep toward the boat, but it was still on the line. I decided to take a moment and call in my first release, so with the bent rod in my left hand, I walked backward toward the salon door, put the boat in neutral, and picked up the radio microphone. The tensed line in my left hand disappeared into the water, just twenty yards behind the port corner of my drifting boat.

"Committee boat, this is boat two thirty-seven."

"Go ahead, two thirty-seven."

"Boat two thirty-seven released a white."

"Two thirty-seven at *one* thirty-seven. Carlos, did you say you tagged the fish?"

"No, no tag in this one, but I am still fighting a second fish."

"OK. No tag . . . one thirty-seven P.M."

I reduced the drag pressure and engaged *Caribeña*'s engine so I could center the line with the marlin in the middle of the transom, well away from the two long rigger lines that were still attached to the outrigger pins and remained in the water. I let out more line from these two reels, one at a time. The closer the fight with the white, the farther away I wanted those two baits. Now I felt I could go on the attack, pumping and reeling, bringing in the line, coil over coil, yard after yard, foot after foot.

Even when I grew as tired as the fish, I still felt in command. When the black line broke the surface a mere ten feet from the boat, I sensed the end and reeled in fast. I had a second release.

But I wanted to tag this marlin before releasing it. I engaged the starboard engine. Facing the wake, I bent the rod in my left hand and grasped the leader with the right. Then I inserted the rod into the rod holder, changed hands, and picked up the tagging pole. The arm motion was short, firm, direct. The tag went in, five or six inches behind the first spine of the rounded dorsal fin. I released the leader and put the boat in motion again in order to keep all the lines straight. The fish was still attached to the leader, swimming along, benefiting from the flow of water going through its open mouth.

Holding the leader, I photographed the fish, then re-moved the hook from its upper jaw. The fish revived, its energy back. Even though I was still holding its bill, its shaking tail let me know it was ready to leave. The marlin seemed surprised when I let it go, and it glided alongside *Caribeña* as if in doubt where to go. Then, it kicked firmly and disap-peared under the cobalt-blue surface of the warm sea.

Still short of breath, I picked up the mike again. "Com-mittee boat," I panted, "this is boat two thirty-seven."

"Go ahead, Carlos."

"Tagged and released. White marlin."

"At one forty-three. Tagged and released. Congratula-tions on your two fish."

"Thanks."

Congratulatory calls came in from friends on different boats. One of them was Dave Care, close by, fishing the Lumps aboard his Albemarle *Careless*. With him were Paul Kingston, who was tied with me as top angler, and also Dave's daughter, Alexis, who took pictures while I was fighting, catching, not tagging, and then tagging the two releases of my second doubleheader of white marlin during this tournament week. Other friends asked and I told them exactly where I was, transmitting the Loran numbers over the airwaves. Within minutes, I was again trolling four baits and the teaser, looking for a white marlin that might reach or exceed seventy-five pounds and put *Caribeña*—and me—at the top of the money board. A dozen or more boats had joined me by now, trying their luck, too, on this offshore southern Lump. But, after my earlier luck, none of us got a strike.

At 3:30 that afternoon, my participation in the twenty-third White Marlin Open Tournament came to an end. Although I was leading in the Released Billfish category, there were still more than 200 boats with one or two days left to hunt for fish, catch them, and beat me.

The ride back to the dock was a trip of some sixty-five nautical miles over calm seas, a pleasant way to unwind. The perfect tournament, I thought to myself. Successive windless days of fishing had brought me a record of five for five. One for one on day one, two for two in each of the two doubleheaders I had on days two and three. I hoisted two inverted white marlin flags to signal that I had released my catch. Twenty feet up on the starboard outrigger halyard, they flapped wildly in the breeze.

This sport being what it is, no official odds are ever posted on any particular boat's chances of success. But it was probably safe to say that, had there been a morning line, *Caribeña* would have been regarded as a long shot in tournament fishing. Logically, she couldn't compete with crews of professional caliber, nor did she have the resources of the fleet's large fishing machines. The fact that I was an underdog may be why I saw so many thumbs-up and so many tipped cap visors above wide smiles as *Caribeña* pulled into the marina. I felt proud.

So did my dockhands. Paul and Johnny were standing side by side on the dock, waving. I backed *Caribeña* into her slip, and the boys handed me the lines. Later I handed my fishing report to Jim and Chuck Motsko, who told me that in the first three days of the tournament, 237 boats had caught fewer than eighty fish.

"*Which* ocean did you fish to come up with this total?" Jim asked. Next to my five white marlin, the next closest angler and boat had, at that point, only two billfish.

The tournament had two more days to run, so I had to wait until Friday night to learn the final results. With a diet soda in my hand, I mingled with the crowd, talking to friends and fellow anglers. Jim and Chuck asked me again to take out the PBS crew that had been taping the tournament. They had gone aboard three different boats, which had, unfortunately, caught no marlin. I was their last hope.

After a day of rest, I set a course toward the outside Lumps of the Washington Canyon as the PBS crew napped most of the way out. Three hours later, I found a promising place, roused them, and, as luck would have it, twenty minutes later *Caribeña* raised and I hooked a white marlin. The crew had what they wanted so badly during the whole week: a jumping marlin on tape.

We came back to port that afternoon to the end of the Open. One thousand three hundred anglers in 237 boats had caught and released 118 white marlin—a low count. John Brown Jr., of Broad Run, Virginia, took home the prize money, fishing on the *Outer Limits*, a boat from Pirate's Cove captained by Harvey Shifflet. Brown caught a white weighing seventy-three pounds, big enough to win $413,890.00—at the time, a world-record purse for a single fish.

The tournament had yielded no monetary rewards, but I couldn't have asked for a better week. My total of 370 billfish points got me named Grand Champion Angler, for which I received a commemorative plaque and a gold Master Ring. I also took home two more Master Rings—for Captain of the Year and Mate of the Year. My *Caribeña*—by then accustomed to this kind of recognition—was crowned the queen of the tournament: Top Boat of 1996.

Even though we had nothing to bring to the scale and convert into gold, we were victorious in defeat. For *Caribeña* and her crew of one, this was the perfect event, where an amalgam of luck, skill, and fate had had its say.

Even so, there was one thing that had always remained unfulfilled for me—and that was the hunt for *El Dentudo*. Five years later, I was roaming one early fall beyond Poor Man's Canyon, seventy-five miles off the Maryland coast, on an unseasonably warm day, where several boats were chunking for tuna with varying degrees of success. I had no interest in tuna: I was intent on finding the last marlin of the season or, perhaps, hooking up with a wahoo, my own *El Dentudo.*

All those years ago, persistent bad weather had kept my mother and me from embarking on our quest to catch Big Tooth, but the image of that fearsome fish and a longing to catch it had stayed with me. I trolled my usual spread of five baits with a small variation. The ballyhoo pulled from the long starboard outrigger was rigged not with mono but thin wire. I also had a one-ounce weight under its chin to keep it submerged. With wire, at least one of my baits would be able to sustain the wahoo's sharp bite.

This fish, from the tribe Scomberomorini, Spanish mackerels, is elongated and torpedo shaped. It resembles both the barracuda and the king mackerel. Like all scombrids, it has small finlets behind the dorsal and anal fins. Wahoo usually weigh thirty to forty pounds, and they are famous for their extraordinarily sharp teeth and great speed.

In the summer and early fall, wahoo roam closer to the mid-Atlantic shore where their bait *du jour*—including sand eels, flying fish, alewives, menhaden, and squid—is abundant between the twenty- and forty-fathom lines. That area holds few marlin, so I rarely fish there—which is probably why I seldom find wahoo attacking my baits. But, later in the season, larger wahoo do run in the deeper water frequented by billfish. In September and October I'm not surprised to have two or three spectacular wahoo bites, but their razor-sharp teeth go through my monofilament leader as if it were spaghetti *al dente*.

This day, however, whether due to kismet or simply luck, a darting V parted the water thirty yards from *Caribeña*'s stern, advancing diagonally to zero in on the wired ballyhoo. Instantly the line snapped from the rigger pin, and an explosive run followed. No splash. No jumps. Just an extremely fast run that made the reel cry. It was clear to me that this was no tuna, marlin, or mahimahi. Tuna splash and go deep, but marlin are usually visible behind the baits and, like mahimahi, once hooked, tend to jump. Experience told me this was a streaking wahoo—an excellent fighter on thirty-pound test. Fifteen minutes later, the fish got closer to *Caribeña*, and I saw its size: just like my mother had said fifty-five years earlier, "That BIG. And with teeth this large!"

More than fifty pounds, I guessed. The wahoo must have sensed the end: it went berserk, shooting away on another fifty-miles-per-hour run, taking 200 yards of line before I could catch my breath. When I brought it close to the transom again, on a second look, it appeared over sixty pounds! This was the crucial moment. I wrapped the wire leader around my gloved left hand with the gaff held high in my right hand. With a fish of this size and strength, I knew how critical my aim was. I would have only one chance to fulfill my boyhood dream. If I missed with the gaff, the wahoo would spook and surge and most probably pull the hook.

I brought the gaff down hard; its sharp point pierced the silvery gill plate at the base of the wahoo's head. I wanted to lift it; it wanted to dive. I summoned strength and hoisted the six-feet brute on board. It was the biggest wahoo I had ever caught—too big to fit in *Caribeña*'s fish box.

That evening back at the dock, the scale registered seventy-five pounds. The wahoo, with its silvery color, black eyes, and big, sharp teeth, fit the image I had been carrying around for fifty-five years. *El Dentudo* had finally been caught.

I intend to keep fishing until I can fish no more. Who knows how long that will be? It may be one, five, or ten years, perhaps longer. But I know that in the not-too-distant future I will have to choose my days, for I may no longer have the physical and mental strength to fish as I do now—braced against the natural elements and probing the metaphysical unknowns that all who venture out into the deep seas confront.

I do love my solitude. I also enjoy spending time with whomever crosses my path, and sometimes, on my solo overnights, I wish that those who I love—my daughter among them—were with me as I gaze up at the heavens. There are joys in life that are magnified when shared with a kindred soul.

I thank my lucky stars, *Las Tres Marias y la Cruz del Sur,* that I have been able to do what I love in the way I have wanted to do it.

Where do we come from: he, the marlin; I, the man? I will keep asking this question as I venture into the unknown. We may be centuries removed from the bone hooks of Cro-Magnon, but the truth is, man keeps fishing for more than fish. I know I do.

ABOUT THE AUTHOR

CARLOS BENTOS is the world's only known championship-winning solo marlin fisherman. Fishing alone, he has won more than thirty competitions, including the annual Ocean City White Marlin Tournament with an unparalleled Super Grand Slam performance. A native Uruguayan, Carlos opened and successfully ran five renowned restaurants in Washington, D.C., for twenty-five years. He is a longtime commentator and writer for Voice of America and has been profiled in publications including *The Washington Post*, *Washingtonian* magazine, *The Baltimore Sun*, *Marlin*, and *Soundings*. Bentos lives in Annapolis, Maryland, and Ocean City, Maryland, where he is at the helm of his new culinary venture, Fathoms Grille, in Sunset Marina. He can be reached on the Internet at www.Caribena.com and www.carlosbentos.com.

ABOUT THE BOAT

CARIBEÑA is the only known sportfishing vessel to have won seven Top Boat annual awards in a decade, which she accomplished while competing against prestigious charter and private boats. There were times when she was underused, mechanically impaired, and even stolen. The author wouldn't have written this book had it not been for her seaworthiness and outstanding performance. She moors year-round in Sunset Marina, in West Ocean City—her bow pointing east.

ACKNOWLEDGMENTS

Writing this book in English was as difficult, pleasurable, and rewarding as running a restaurant, catching a large marlin, or bringing a boat safe to port during a scary storm. And perhaps more so, for, while accustomed to act alone in the course of the last three endeavors, writing involved having a "crew" offering suggestions or making decisions about the right approach, or plotting the proper course for this book.

It was two decades ago that Vivian Herder, an internationally accomplished deep-sea angler in the 60s and 70s, first mentioned that I should write a book about my solitary fishing. More recently, my good friend Joe Barse, the designated historian of the Ocean City Light Tackle Club, read some of the original drafts and encouraged me to continue this work. He offered suggestions and shared information on the history of billfishing and tagging, which I partially used in this book. Elizabeth Stone, Irish Dove Britell, Cecilia Umanzor, Lisa Kadous, Val Lynch, and Marta Braunstein also read and commented on some of the early chapters. Capt. Joe Riley introduced me to the parents and family of Chris Bowie, and all shared thoughts and emotions while revisiting a tragic time in their lives. Sarah Jane Freymann, one of the two literary agents I queried after I had received a publisher's offer, believed in this book. And so did Wendy Hubbert, the senior editor at Tarcher/Putnam, who first acquired the English rights to this work and later worked closely with Kenny Wapner, restructuring, shuffling, and editing chapters and passages of my original, more lyrical manuscript. Allison Sobel, editorial assistant at Tarcher, and Carol Rosenberg, copyeditor at Penguin Putnam, both did a wonderful, thorough job. Thanks to Kelly Groves and Kristen Giorgio. To all—without correlation—for their interest, time, patience, suggestions, friendship, love, kindness, humor, effort, help, insight, and actual support, a shipload of genuine gratitude.